The Reason I Created
MECCA

Shadae Jenkins Bell

Lawyer:
University of San Francisco School of Law

Elijah Jenkins

Lawyer:
Howard University School of Law

Eden Jenkins

Doctor of Pharmacy (PharmD)
Student Xavier University of Louisiana
(Class of 2024) & PXU Million Dollar Scholar

Jahson Jenkins

Employment/Workforce & Phoenix College Student
(Class of 2024) EMT Certification

MECCA
THE ONE-STOP SHOP FOR ALL YOUR COLLEGE ADMISSIONS NEEDS

MECCA College ADMISSIONS Playbook & Guide

ISBN:
979-8-9907357-0-5

Front cover image by Artist: Fishy Graphx

Printed by Fishy Graphx
Printed in the United States

First printing edition 2024

Publisher: Self-Published (Sandra McKnight)

www.meccacollegeadmissionshelp.com

MECCA College ADMISSIONS Playbook & Guide

INTRODUCTION

The MECCA College Admissions Playbook and Guide is information and resources that will help equip students with the knowledge needed to confidently select, prepare, apply, enroll and succeed in college.

Leaders of counseling for college and career readiness find that providing information and support to parents is essential for helping students and their families plan for post-graduation. While parents hold high expectations for their children's higher education and careers, they may not necessarily be equipped with the resources needed to help guide their children for these transitions.

McKnight Educational Consulting for College Admissions (MECCA) is committed to working directly with underrepresented students of color to:

- increase academic performance and post-secondary preparation
- increase high school graduation and postsecondary enrollment rates
- increase educational expectations for students
- increase knowledge of postsecondary options for students and families.

MECCA provides targeted programming, resources, and pertinent information to assist families in navigating the entire college admissions process.

TABLE OF CONTENTS

Student Personal Information

Take a few minutes to fill out this form. Then with your high school transcript and ECAP (Educational and Career Action Plan) in hand, you'll have everything you need to complete most college applications. You might need to work with your parents or family members to get all the details.

Contact Information

Full Name (first, middle, last)	
Street Address	
PO Box	
City, State, Zip Code	
Home Phone Number	
Mobile Phone Number	
Email Address (not your high school email address)	
Social Security Number	
Driver's License Number and Date Issued	
Date of Birth / Gender	

School Information

Name of Current High School	
Street Address, City, State, Zip Code	
Telephone Number	
Expected Graduation Date	
Name of Previous High School Attended	
Street Address, City, State, Zip Code	
Telephone Number	
Dates Attended	
Classification or Grade Level (circle one)	Freshman Sophomore Junior Senior

GPA and Testing (ACT, SAT, AP, CLEP, & placement test)

Weighted GPA			Unweighted GPA		
SAT Date (month / year)			Comp Score		
ACT Date (month / year)			Comp Score		
AP Subject		Score	AP Subject		Score
AP Subject		Score	AP Subject		Score
CLEP Subject		Score	CLEP Subject		Score
IB		Score	IB		Score
College Placement / Accuplacer		Date(s)	Subject / Score		

Student Personal Information

Athletics, Clubs, Organizations, and Leadership

Club / Sports Team	List your role / position each year			
	Freshman	Sophomore	Junior	Senior

Honors & Awards

Name and Date of Award	Reason for Award / Honor	Sponsor

Community Service

Name of the organization	Description of volunteer service	Dates of service	Number of hours of service	Take-aways: What you learned, enjoyed, experienced	Name of contact and contact information (email, phone, website, and / or address}

Emergency Contact

Name / Relationship:	
Phone Number	
Address	

MECCA College Awareness Pre-Assessment

This assessment will help you determine your present level of knowledge regarding some of the topics related to getting ready for college.

Decide how much you agree or disagree with each statement. Circle and write your rating.

Statement	Strongly Agree	Agree	Neutral	Disagree	Strongly Disagree	My Rating
	Rating Scale		Choose a number on the left to agree or on the right to disagree.			
I should take challenging courses (including Advanced Placement [AP], Inter-national Baccalaureate [18] and dual credit and honors if offered.)	5	4	3	2	1	
I am extremely comfortable navigating the college admissions process with little to no assistance.	1	2	3	4	5	
I should stay in contact with my school counselor about resources for college.	5	4	3	2	1	
I plan to apply to one college for admission.	1	2	3	4	5	
I should volunteer and get involved in extracurricular activities.	5	4	3	2	1	
I am familiar with all college applications.	1	2	3	4	5	
I should develop relationships with teachers, coaches, mentors, or other adults, as they will provide recommendation letters.	5	4	3	2	1	
I know I can only apply to colleges and universities using online applications.	1	2	3	4	5	
I should begin early to research scholarships and other funding opportunities.	5	4	3	2	1	
I will only apply to colleges and universities I can afford.	1	2	3	4	5	
Thoroughly research colleges and majors to find the right fit for you and your future career goals.	5	4	3	2	1	
No other materials are required with my college application.	1	2	3	4	5	
Talk to your school counselor about any college fairs or universities visiting your high school or offering virtual fairs.	5	4	3	2	1	
I will need to declare a major before I apply to a college or university.	1	2	3	4	5	
Some applications can be disqualified simply because students do not submit all the required documents.	5	4	3	2	1	
I should apply for financial aid only if I believe I qualify.	1	2	3	4	5	
Seek college application and testing fee waivers from organizations and colleges.	5	4	3	2	1	
My parents' tax return has nothing to do with my dependency status.	1	2	3	4	5	
Create folders (virtual or hard copy) for each college application and/ or create a college application spreadsheet.	5	4	3	2	1	
I should not apply to a college or university if my GPA and ACT/SAT test scores are below the school's entrance requirements.	1	2	3	4	5	

Add the numbers and write the total.

90 -100 **CONFIDENT** about college readiness preparation	70-89 **COMFORTABLE** about college readiness preparation	50-69 **CURIOUS** about college readiness preparation	0-49 **CONFUSED** about college readiness preparation

Identify Your Passions

Interests revolve around things you like to do, and passions involve strong feelings you hold about certain subjects. For instance, people who work in healthcare often get into that career because they're passionate about helping people heal. If you consider your interests and honor your passions, they will lead you to lots of career options. So, let's identify some subject areas you're passionate about to help build self-awareness.

Instructions: Review the list below and circle two to four topics you know about personally or indirectly, from the news, or even through social media that get you excited, spark curiosity, or make you want to change something about them.

• Access to healthcare/healthcare reform	• Foster care
• Access to quality childcare	• Health & fitness
• Access to technology/internet	• Homelessness
• Animals	• Income inequality
• Art	• Literacy
• Banking	• Mental illness/mental health
• Better technology (quieter, cheaper, lighter}	• Migrants/immigrants
• Carpentry	• Military veterans' reintegration
• Children's rights	• Music
• Civil rights/discrimination	• Obesity
• Climate change	• Poverty
• College access for everyone	• Quality education for all
• Disease	• Reduce/reuse/recycle
• Design	• Renewable energy
• Entrepreneurship	• Sports
• Environmental protection	• Substance abuse/alcoholism
• Equity and justice	• Teaching
• Faith	• Hybrid/electric transportation
• Finance/insurance	• Workers' rights/fair pay

Adapted from: https://in.nau.edu/gear-up/discover-guide/

Identify Your Abilities

If you plan to enter the workforce immediately after high school graduation, then this checklist is for you!

Ability	Description	Score		
Mechanical	I can take things apart and put them back together to see how they work.	1	2	3
Scientific	I understand the way people, technology, and the environment connect.	1	2	3
Artistic	I find it easy to draw, paint, act, dance, or create something new.	1	2	3
Teaching	I can help others learn new things.	1	2	3
Sales	I can sway friends to join in something fun.	1	2	3
Organizational	I plan, prioritize, and manage school and free time activities to achieve goals.	1	2	3
Writing	I like to write about life, create stories, or persuade others with reports and speeches.	1	2	3
Reading	I apply what I read to other areas of my life, and I understand fact from fiction.	1	2	3
Language	I understand correct grammar and use it.	1	2	3
Spatial Perception	I look at drawings and "see" the object from different points of view.	1	2	3
Understanding Others	I can get along with others and recognize their point of view; I make a good first impression.	1	2	3
Helping Others	I show support or lend a hand when friends share problems.	1	2	3
Leadership	I can enlist the help of others to work toward a common goal.	1	2	3
Math	I apply math concepts to resolve problems; I'm good with numbers.	1	2	3

Adapted from: https://www.change-management-coach.com/aptitude-test.html

Abilities you rated as a 2 or 3 show where your natural skills shine. Careers that require those abilities will bring you more pleasure because these skills come easily to you.

career exploration sites
https://www.xello.world/en/
https://bigfuture.collegeboard.org/explore-careers#!
https://www.mynextmove.org/explore/ip

Learning Style Quiz

https://www.tamuk.edu/academicaffairssupport/teaching-effectiveness/_ftles_CTE/faculty-toolkit/LearningStyleQuiz.pdf

What is your learning style? Look back over how you have learned best in the past; you can make informed choices about the kind of program you choose to enroll in. Read the following questions and circle the letter of the best answer in your opinion. There are no right or wrong answers. Just circle what you usually prefer.

1. When learning how to use my computer, I prefer to:
   A. Read the manual first
   B. Have someone explain how to do it first
   C. Just start using the computer and get help if I need it

2. When getting directions to a new location, it is easier to:
   A. Look at a map
   B. Have someone tell me how to get there
   C. Follow someone or have them take me there

3. To remember a phone number, I:
   A. Look at the number and dial it several times
   B. Repeat it silently or out loud to myself several times
   C. Remember the number by the pattern pressed on the keypad, the tones of each number or by writing it down

4. For relaxation, I prefer to:
   A. Read a book or magazine
   B. Listen to or play music
   C. Go for a walk or do something physical

5. I am better at:
   A. Reading
   B. Talking
   C. Physical activities

6. In school, I learn best by:
   A. Reading
   B. Listening
   C. Hands-on activities

7. I tend to be a:
   A. Thinker
   B. Talker
   C. Doer

8. It is easier for me to remember:
   A. Faces
   B. Names
   C. Events

9. On Saturday, I would prefer to:
   A. See a movie
   B. Go to a concert
   C. Participate in athletics or be outside

10. In a college class, it is most important to have:
    A. A good textbook with pictures, graphs and diagrams
    B. A good teacher who has interesting lectures
    C. Hands-on activities

11. It is easier to study by:
    A. Reading and reviewing the material
    B. Discussing the subject with others
    C. Writing notes or outlines

12. When I get lost, I prefer to:
    A. Look at the map
    B. Call or ask for directions
    C. Drive around the area until I recognize familiar landmarks

13. When cooking, I often:
    A. Look for new recipes
    B. Talk to others to get new ideas
    C. Put it together and it generally comes out OK

14. When solving a problem, it is more useful to:
    A. Read a best-selling book on the topic
    B. Talk over the options with a trusted friend
    C. Do something about it

Score Your Quiz:

Visual Learners _____ Count your number of A's above.

Auditory Learners _____ Count your number of B's above.

Kinesthetic/Hands on Learners _____ Count your number of C's above

Family, Community, and Cultural Influences

Personal abilities and passions make you unique and bring self-awareness, which will help guide you about careers you may want to pursue. In addition, your family, community, and culture shape your values and beliefs, which also play a role in choosing the right career. This activity will show you how you feel about these influences.

Instructions: Rate the statements below-there are no wrong answers.

I want to share my career, dreams, and goals with my family and friends.	1	2	3
I want to pursue the same career as a family member because of tradition.	1	2	3
I want my parents/guardian to approve of my career path.	1	2	3
My family's (parents) opinions about my career path are important.	1	2	3
Calculate the average to get your family influence rating here.	**Add Total Points**	**+4=**	**_____**

I want to pursue a career highly regarded in my community.	1	2	3
I want to choose a job where I can serve my community.	1	2	3
My cultural identity will play an important role in the career I choose.	1	2	3
I want to incorporate my cultural traditions in my career.	1	2	3
Calculate the average to get your community/culture influence rating here.	**Add Total Points ____**	**+ 4 =**	

My life experiences motivate me to pursue a certain career.	1	2	3
My observations about friends or the world motivate me to pursue certain careers.	1	2	3
Calculate the average to get your experiences influence rating here.	**Add Total Points ___**	**+ 2 =**	

Adapted from: https://in.nau.edu/gear-up/discover-guide/

Mental Wellness Resources

Mental wellness resources for students to seek support could be the key to academic success.

CRISIS SERVICES

Suicide and Crisis Hotline (24/7): 9-8-8

Crisis Response Network (24/7): 602-222-9444

Mind 24/7 (Urgent Psychiatric Care): 1-844-646-3247

St. Luke's Behavioral Health (Psychiatric Hospital): 602-251-8535

Teen Lifeline (24/7 free service with trained peer counselors): 602-248-8336

Safe Place (24/7 help for youth in trouble): 602-841-5799

Arizona Department of Child Safety: 1-888-SOS-CHILD (1-888-767-2445)

Phoenix Police Crimestop (non-emergency): 602-262-6151

COUNSELING

Bayless Integrated Healthcare: 602-230-7373

Chicanos Por La Causa: 623-247-0464

Charlie Health (virtual counseling services): 866-491-5196

Jewish Family and Children Service: 602-256-0528

La Frontera (counseling, crisis, housing): 480-784-1514 ext. 1048

Native American Connections (counseling, housing, economic): 602-424-2060

Native Health (AHCCCS or self-pay): 602-279-5262

New Song (grief support) 480-951-8985

One-n-Ten (LGBTQ youth support): 602-279-0894

Phoenix Indian Medical Center (medical & behavioral health services for tribal members): 602-263-1200

COUNSELING

Southwest Behavioral & Health Services:602-265-8338

House of Miracles, Inc. 623-203-7381

University of Phoenix (free counseling services provided by graduate level students): 480-557-2217

Valle Del Sol (case management, counseling & psych evaluation): 602-523-9312

ASSISTANCE

AHCCCS/KidsCare: 1-800-564-5465

ALWAYS (free legal advice & services for women & youth): 602-248-7055

Domestic Violence / Homeless Shelter Hotline: 1-800-352-3792

Friendly House (education, workforce development, family services, & immigration services): 602-257-1870

HomeBase Youth Services (transitional housing for youth aged 18-24): 602-263-5531

Homeless Youth Connection (host families, basic needs & services): 623-374-3747 / After hours: 602-633-4844

Maryvale Health Center: 623-344-6900 4011 B, 51st Ave., Phoenix

Mission of Mercy (free primary medical care): 602-861-2233

Phoenix Job Corps: 800-733-5627

Runaway Hotline (support for runaway, homeless & at-risk youth: 1-800-RUNAWAY (1-800-786-2929)

St. Mary's Food Bank (emergency food boxes): 602-242-3663; 3131 W. Thomas Rd., Phoenix

TASC (treatment, counseling & drug screening): 602-254-7328

Setting Life Goals

For each category listed below, write one or more goals. Then list the actions and the commitment costs it will take to reach your goals

Category	My Goals	Actions	Commitment Costs
Family	1.	1.	1.
	2.	2.	2.
	3.	3.	3.
Key Relationships	1.	1.	1.
	2.	2.	2.
	3.	3.	3.
Spiritual	1.	1.	1.
	2.	2.	2.
	3.	3.	3.
Physical Health	1.	1.	1.
	2.	2.	2.
	3.	3.	3.
Personal and Mental Health	1.	1.	1.
	2.	2.	2.
	3.	3.	3.
Community	1.	1.	1.
	2.	2.	2.
Business	1.	1.	1.
	2.	2.	2.

DIFFERENCE BETWEEN
HIGH SCHOOL AND COLLEGE

HIGH SCHOOL		COLLEGE
At least 30 hours per week of classroom instruction.	SCHEDULE	Usually, 12 to 17 hours per week of classroom instruction.
Students' time and schedule is structured in most parts by others.		Students manage their own time and register for their own classes.
Small classes, usually no more than 35 students/class.	CLASS SIZE	Larger lecture classes, sometimes with hundreds of students
Textbooks are provided at no cost.	TEXTBOOKS	College textbooks are paid by the student and can be expensive.
Grades are given for most assigned work.	GRADES	Grades may not be provided for all assigned work.
"Effort counts." Courses are usually structured to reward a "good-faith effort."		"Results count." Though "good-faith effort" is important, it will not substitute for results in the grading process.
Bells ring to tell students when to go to the next class and students must study all subjects.	CLASSES	Students are responsible for being on time for class. Students have more flexibility in what they study.
Students are told in class what they need to learn from assigned readings.		It's up to the student to read and understand the assigned material.
Instructors are called teachers. Teachers are available for conversations before, during, or after class.	TEACHER-STUDENT CONTACT	Instructors are called professors. Professors expect and want you to attend their scheduled office hours.
Teachers bear much of the responsibility for your learning.		You bear the responsibility for your learning while your professors serve as guides, mentors, and resources.
Personalized counseling by teachers and guidance counselors; help from parents/legal guardians.	ACADEMIC SUPPORT	Requested and arranged by the student. Students are responsible for registration.
More frequent with tests at the end of each unit or quarter.	TESTS	Tests are infrequent and cumulative, covering large amounts of material.
Mastery is usually seen as the ability to reproduce what you were taught in the form in which it was presented to you.		Mastery is seen as the ability to apply what you've learned to new situations or to solve new kinds of problems.
Routines are established and enforced by parents, school community traditions.	INDEPENDENCE	Students must establish schedules and maintain their own routines.
Student's status in academic and social situations is often influenced by family and community factors.	STATUS	The student is judged solely for themselves and by their own behavior and actions.
Students are usually told what to do and corrected if their behavior is not in line with set expectations.	DEPENDENCE	Students must take responsibility for their own path and academic success, as well as the consequences and rewards of their actions.

College Tips Every Student Should Follow

- Attend All Classes
- Avoid Being Distracted by Social Media
- Avoid Procrastinating or Waiting to Start Assignments
- Monitor Your Health (Mental and Physical)
- Make Friends
- Ask for Help When Needed
- Join Clubs on Campus
- Attend Campus Events
- Budget Time Wisely (time management)
- Budget Money Wisely
- Beware of Dating APPs
- Stay Focused
- Search for Scholarships, Work Study, and Grants Opportunities
- Search for Study Abroad Opportunities
- Search for Job and Intern Opportunities
- Submit FAFSA Application Each Year
- Learn to Share a Living Space with a Roommate
- Schedule "Down" Time
- Find a Mentor/Accept Support
- Learn to Handle Conflict Resolution with Compassion and Empathy

Soft Skills & Social Skills Needed for College

- Self-Advocacy
- Self-Care
- Digital Citizenship & Safety
- Communication
- Collaboration
- Time Management/Punctuality
- Customer Service
- Keeping an Open Mind
- Integrity/Acting Honestly
- Maintaining Composure/Self-Control
- Socializing with Others
- Getting Along with Others
- Sustaining Effort
- Self-Confidence
- Empathy
- Curiosity
- Perseverance
- Optimism

Productivity Apps & Websites:

- Evernote (https://evernote.com/)
- MyStudyLife (https://mystudylife.com/)
- Habitica (https://habitica.com/static/home)
- Cold Turkey (https://getcoldturkey.com/)
- SelfControl (Mac) (https://selfcontrolapp.com/)
- myHomework (https://myhomeworkapp.com/)

Stress Management Apps:

- Breathr: A Mindfulness App (https://keltymentalhealth.ca/breathr)
- Calm (https://www.calm.com/)
- Dare (https://apps.apple.com/us/app/dare-panic-anxiety-relief/id1034311206)
- Headspace (https://www.headspace.com/headspace-meditation-app)
- Happify (https://www.happify.com)
- InsightTimer (https://insighttimer.com/)
- MindShift (https://www.anxietycanada.com/resources/mindshift-cbt/)
- Smiling Mind (https://www.smilingmind.com.au/)
- Headspace (https://www.headspace.com/)
- Breethe (https://breethe.com/)

Develop Your Career Personality

This activity takes your interests and abilities into account as you prioritize the activities you like. Then, you'll take this information to discover what careers use the kinds of interests and activities that you enjoy. Record the letters from the three "top" scores below. 1. 2. 3.

STEP 1. Identify Your Career Code

Below, **circle** all the activities that appeal to you and total them in each box.

1. **Count** the items you circled in each box and record the number at the bottom of each box.
2. **Record** the letters you circled from the three "top" scores below.

R	I	A

• Farming
• Auto mechanics
• Carpentry
• Wildlife biology
• Building things
• Electronics repair
• Driving a truck
	• Advanced math
	• Astronomy Physics
	• Using a chemistry set
	• Being in a science fair
	• Doing puzzles
	• Building rocket models
	• Working in a science lab
		• Acting in a play
		• Drawing or painting
		• Playing an instrument
		• Learning foreign languages
		  Reading about art or music
		  Going to concerts
		• Designing clothing
		• Writing for enjoyment

Total R =_____	Total I = _____	Total A = _____
S	**E**	**C**
• Helping people • Community service • Teaching children • Studying foreign cultures • Making new friends • Attending sports events • Belonging to a club • Working with elderly people	• Selling a product • Being with leaders • Giving speeches • Talking with people at a party • Working on a sales campaign • Buying materials for a store • Being elected class president • Talking to salespeople	• Using a cash register • Following a budget • Using business machines • Keeping detailed reports • Typing on a computer • Filing letters and reports • Working in a systematic, orderly way
Total S =_____	Total E =_____	Total C = _____

Adapted from: https://in.nau.edu/gear-up/discover-guide/

Record the letters from the three "top" scores below.

1. _____   2. ....   3. ....

STEP 2. Match Your Interests

Instructions: Take your top three scores from the previous page and find potential career opportunities that match your interests.

Realistic people have
athletic or mechanical abilities. They usually like to work outdoors with objects, machines, tools, plants, or animals.

- Auto body repair
- Electrician
- Firefighter
- Farmer
- Cabinet maker
- Mechanic
- Commercial driver
- Surveyor
- Mechanical engineer

Investigative people like to
observe, learn, investigate, analyze, or solve problems.

- Engineer
- Chemist
- Fire investigator
- Biologist
- Veterinarian
- Doctor
- Environmental scientist
- Information security analyst

Artistic people have
innovative or intuitive abilities. They usually like to work in an unstructured situation, using their imagination and creativity.

- Actor/actress
- Architect
- Interior decorator
- Composer
- Dancer
- Musician
- Stage director
- Writer

Social people like to work
with others. They like to inform, enlighten, help, train, develop, or cure people. They may be skilled with words.

- Psychologist
- Physical therapist
- Teacher
- Speech therapist
- Counselor
- Athletic trainer
- Dental hygienist

Enterprising people like to
work with people, but they like to influence, persuade, or perform. They like to lead or manage for organizational goals or economic gain.

- Salesperson
- Buyer
- Flight attendant
- Manager
- Travel agent
- Lawyer
- Cosmetologist

Conventional people like to
work with data, have clerical or numerical ability, and pay attention to detail.

- Air traffic controller
- Accountant
- Receptionist
- Administrator
- Financial analyst
- Mail carrier
- Court reporter
- Computer operator

Reflection

What job seems like a good fit based on the types of activities you enjoy? _____

_____

Were you surprised by any of your findings? _____

What did you learn about career personalities and job types that could be a good fit? _____

_____

Career Interest Survey/Assessment

In order to choose a career that will give your personal satisfaction, you must spend some time thinking about what really interests you. Please click on the Career Assessment links below to explore career interests: www.careeronestop.org, www.mynextmove.org, and https://xello.world/en/. They ask a series of short questions and is designed for use on computers, smartphones, or tablets.

Agriculture, Animals and Natural Resources
Agricultural Engineer
Animal Trainer
Chef
Farm Equipment Mechanic
Fish and Game Warden
Forester
Veterinarian
Zoologist

Architecture and Construction
Architect
Cabinetmaker
Carpenter
Electrician
Civil Engineer
General Construction Worker
Interior Designer
Sheet Metal Worker

Arts, A/V Technology and Communications
Actor
Art Director
Broadcast Technician
Camera Operator
Composer and Music Arranger
Film and Video Editor
Cartographer
News Reporter
Photographer
Producer and Director
Set and Exhibit Designer
Graphic Designer

Business, Management and Administration
Accountant
Advertising Manager
Computer Operator
Court Reporter
Management Analyst
Meeting and Convention Planner
Payroll Clerk
Property and Real Estate Manager
Statistician

Education and Training
Audiovisual Specialist
Coach and Sports Instructor
College/University Administrator
Teacher/Professor
Librarian
Public Health Educator
Special Education Teacher

Finance
Accounting Clerk
Economist
Financial Counselor
Insurance Adjuster and Examiner
Insurance Agent
Tax Preparer

Government and Public Administration
City Planning Aide
Construction/Building Inspector
Interpreter and Translator
Occupational Health Specialist
Tax Examiner

Health Sciences
Anesthesiologist
Athletic Trainer
Chiropractor
Dentist
Emergency Medical Technician
Physical Therapist
Pharmacist
Physician
Registered Nurse

Hospitality and Tourism
Chef and Dinner Cook
Food Service Worker
Hotel Manager
Janitor/Housekeeper Supervisor
Restaurant Manager
Travel Agent
Umpire and Referee

Human Services
Childcare Worker
Cosmetologist
Counselor
Funeral Director
Manicurist
Financial Adviser
Psychologist
Social Worker

Information Technology (IT)
Computer/Information Systems Manager
Computer Engineer
Computer Programmer
Computer Security Specialist
Computer Systems Analyst
Data Communications Analyst
IT Mechanic

Law, Public Safety, Corrections and Security
Coroner
Corrections Officer
Court Clerk
Detective and Investigator
Firefighter
Judge
Lawyer
Police Patrol Officer

Manufacturing (Mechanical/Industrial)
Chemical Engineer
Forklift Operator
Gas and Oil Plant Operator
Jeweler
Locksmith
Metal/Plastic Processing Worker
Power Plant Operator
Shoe and Leather Worker
Welder

Marketing, Sales and Services
Advertising Salesperson
Buyer and Purchasing Agent
Customer Service Representative
Floral Designer
Market Research Analyst
Public Relations Specialist
Real Estate Agent
Sales Manager
Telemarketer

Science, Technology, Engineering and Mathematics
Aerospace Engineer
Biologist
Chemist
Electrical and Electronics Engineer
Geographer
Petroleum Engineer
Mechanical Engineer
Meteorologist
Physicist
Safety Engineer

Transportation, Distribution and Logistics
Air Traffic Controller
Airplane Pilot
Automobile Mechanic
Flight Attendant
Motorboat Mechanic
School Bus Driver

Education & Career Action Plan (ECAP)

Explore Interests, Passions, Abilities, and Influences

The top three interests that spark curiosity and inspire me to learn more:		
Three of my passions are:		
I'm good at all sorts of things, but I can imagine using the skills and abilities below most frequently in my career:		
Considering family, community and cultural values is important to me. {Circle one} Yes No		

This Is Where I Want to Go

Based on my explorations so far, the following career cluster seems like the best fit:	
The three specific careers in that cluster that interest me the most:	

Academic Preparation

In-School (Curricular)							
My grades from my most recent report cards:							
English		Math		Social Studies		Science	
Looking at my grades, I need to improve: Math, Science, English, and Social Studies.							
English		Math		Social Studies		Science	

During high school, besides Math, Science, English, and Social Studies, I may need to take these courses for my ideal career:

1.	3.
2.	4.

Outside of School (Extracurricular)	

After-school activities or organizations in my community that would be fun to explore and could help me develop job skills.

1.	2.

This Is How I Will Get There

The credential I need for my ideal career/occupation is:
____ Certificate ____ Associate Degree ____ Bachelor's Degree ____ Professional Degree License
The pathway through which I can get this credential {check one or more}:
__University __ Community __ College __ Apprenticeship __Technical Institute __ Military
List experiences you can seek out, beyond education, to help you prepare for college and career:

Adapted from: https://in.nau.edu/gear-up/discover-guide/

Career Research Project

Career Research Project Topics	Career Information
CAREER Career Name:	
Post-Secondary Education Required (What major and degree level)	
School or Training/post-secondary choices (Where would you attend school?)	
WORK VALUES & PASSIONS (WV & P) (WV=Helping others, taking risks)	
(P= Learning something new, being true to self)	
SMART GOALS Long-Term Professional Goal	
Long-Term Personal Goal	
IMPLEMENTATION What type of Industry would you work in?	
What type of Companies would you work for?	
Work part-time or full-time	
Work 1 job or 2 jobs	
MY BUDGET PROFILE – Will you have enough to cover your expenses? (Budget Activity, what is your total projected yearly salary, the average/median yearly wages of the job you chose) Explain how you will cope if there is not enough money.	
JOB DUTIES (5 job duties/daily tasks)	
DRESS AND SAFETY EQUIPMENT What will you wear to work? What tools or safety gear will you use?	
TYPICAL WORKDAY (describe)	

College Readiness Checklist & Timeline by Grade Level

8th Grade Checklist

- ✓ Think about college as an important part of your future. Discuss your thoughts and ideas with your family, counselor and teachers.
- ✓ Start saving for college if you haven't already.
- ✓ Take challenging courses to prepare for high school.
- ✓ Ask your parent or guardian to help you research which special programs will most benefit your interests.
- ✓ Speak with adults, such as your parents, teacher, school counselor, or other relatives, who you think have interesting jobs and ask them what education they needed for their job.
- ✓ Spring of eighth grade is an excellent time to map out a proposed four-year plan for high school.
- ✓ Colleges and scholarship committees like to see well-rounded, active students. Students who are involved in activities seem to enjoy high school more and generally have greater academic success. Eighth graders should enter the ninth grade ready to "sign up" for activities that they will enjoy and that will make each participating student a more important part of the high school community.

9th Grade Checklist

- ✓ Set goals (personal, professional, behavior, family, relationships, spiritual, physical, and community)
- ✓ Meet and get to know your high school Guidance Counselor
- ✓ Practice good study habits and earn good grades
- ✓ Get involved in activities, sports, and clubs on your campus
- ✓ Look for Community service and volunteer opportunities to help build your resume
- ✓ Take multiple Career Aptitude Surveys to help you determine your interests, college and career goals
- ✓ Attend tutoring when necessary
- ✓ Start exploring colleges you may be interested in attending
- ✓ Review student athlete eligibility requirements
- ✓ Read as much as possible to help build vocabulary, prepare for aptitude tests, and learn new ideas
- ✓ Practice your writing skills using prompts or free style to help develop your voice and prepare you for college essays later
- ✓ Register for summer programs or take additional academic courses

College Readiness Checklist & Timeline by Grade Level

10th Grade Checklist

- ✓ Ask your Guidance Counselor to enroll you in rigorous courses to help prepare you for college and discuss graduation requirements, future classes and goals
- ✓ Maintain good grades
- ✓ Attend tutoring when necessary
- ✓ Register for the Pre-SAT (PSAT) Test and Pre-ACT (PLAN) Test, if offered at your school, to get an idea of what to expect when you take the actual ACT/SAT Tests
- ✓ Find an ACT/SAT Prep Program online or in your school community
- ✓ Familiarize yourself with the basic college entrance requirements and the college admissions process
- ✓ Continue to research careers and schools that interest you
- ✓ Create a balanced list of schools that fit your interests: safety, match, and reach
- ✓ Continue your participation with extracurricular activities
- ✓ Continue to practice reading and writing in your spare time to help prepare you for college entrance exams and admission essays
- ✓ Plan college visits (virtual or in-person)
- ✓ Attend College Fairs

11th Grade Checklist

- ✓ Meet with Guidance Counselor to ensure you're on track for graduation, monitor GPA, and class rank
- ✓ Focus on maintaining good grades
- ✓ Attend tutoring when necessary
- ✓ Register for the PSAT in October
- ✓ Review admission requirements for colleges/universities on your school list
- ✓ Stay engaged in extracurricular activities and prepare for a leadership role in sports, clubs, etc.
- ✓ Enroll in an ACT/SAT Prep Program online or in your school community
- ✓ Review ACT/SAT Test dates, register and request a fee waiver from your Guidance Counselor
- ✓ Start building relationships with educators who can write a letter of recommendation for you
- ✓ Attend College Fairs and Information Sessions
- ✓ Continue to plan college tours (virtually or in-person)
- ✓ Research scholarship opportunities
- ✓ Narrow down your college list: safety, match, and reach
- ✓ Enroll in summer programs/classes, secure a job or internship
- ✓ Start brainstorming or drafting ideas for your college essays and search for essay prompts from previous years

12th Grade Checklist

- ✓ Meet with your high school Guidance Counselor to review your academic status, remaining credits to complete, request letter of recommendation, and discuss post-secondary goals
- ✓ Retake ACT/SAT to improve your score and release scores to all school on your list
- ✓ Stay organized
- ✓ Complete college applications
- ✓ Create a resume
- ✓ Request letters of recommendation from counselors, teachers, coaches, club sponsors, community organizations, etc.
- ✓ Create a college portfolio
- ✓ Finalize college list: safety, match, and reach
- ✓ Continue to attend College Fairs and Informational Sessions
- ✓ Continue to plan college visits {virtually and in-person)
- ✓ Complete the FAFSA as early as October 1st
- ✓ Verify that all materials were received by prospective colleges/universities on your school list {applications, letters of recommendation, transcripts, ACT/SAT scores, financial aid, immunization/health records, NCAA or NAIA Eligibility status, etc.)
- ✓ Apply for multiple scholarships
- ✓ Review and compare financial aid packages and acceptance letters
- ✓ Choose a college or university

High School Transcripts

- These will be sent after you submit your college application online
- Before you graduate you must request a final transcript be sent to the college you will be attending
- These may include scores of tests you took while in high school {ACT/SAT)

Health Records & Immunization

- You will need to furnish your health records to your college or university
- Required health records include the General Health Form, Mandatory Immunization Record Verification Form, and Mandatory Physical Exam Form
- All forms must be completed and signed by a licensed Physician or Nurse Practitioner
- These may be obtained from the Health Center at your high school or from your doctor

Student Athletes

- To compete at the college level, the NCAA Clearinghouse Application or the NAIA Application must be completed
- Forms are on their websites at www.ncaaclearinghouse.net or www.naia.org
- Send admission applications to the college admissions office not the athletic office
- ACT or SAT scores are required for college athletes

ACT vs. SAT

ACT	SAT
Total Time	
2 hours, 55 minutes (without writing) 3 hours, 35 minutes (with writing)	3 hours (without essay) 3 hours, 50 minutes (with essay)
Subjects and Time (in order they appear on test)	
1. English: 45 mins, 75 questions 2. Math: 60 mins, 60 questions 3. Reading: 35 mins, 40 questions 4. Science: 35 mins, 40 questions 5. Writing (optional): 40 mins, 1 essay	1. Reading: 65 mins, 52 questions 2. Writing and Language: 35 mins, 44 questions 3. Math: 80 mins, 58 questions 4. Essay (optional): 50 mins, 1 essay
Tools	
You can use a calculator on all math questions.	Some math questions don't allow you to use a calculator.
Essay	
Optional. Essay assesses your writing skills and your ability to compare and contrast different perspectives. For the essay, you will read a short passage about an issue and then analyze the different perspectives on this issue. You'll be asked to give your own opinion on the issue.	Optional. Essay assesses your writing skills and your reading comprehension skills. For the essay, you will read a short passage about an issue. Your essay will analyze the author's argument using evidence and reasoning. In other words, you will not be giving your own opinion.
Score	
Total score range: 1 - 36 Each section uses a scale of 1 – 36. Your total score is the average of your four section scores. The optional Writing section uses a scale of 2 - 12 and does not count toward your final score.	**Total score range: 400 - 1600** The Evidence-Based Reading and Writing (EBRW) and Math sections each use a scale of 200 – 800 and are combined for a total score. The optional Essay uses three separate scales of 2 - 8 and does not count toward your final score.
Accommodations	
English Learners and students with documented disabilities can request accommodations.	Students with disabilities can request accommodations.
Registration and Preparation Tools available at:	
www.act.org/	satsuite.collegeboard.org/sa

College Research Project

Researching Postgraduate Educ. (University/College/Vocational/Technical Schools)

1. SCHOOL	School Name and Address and Contact Information

2. At a Glance

- Urban or Rural: _____
- Undergraduate Students: _____
- Admissions: _____
- In-state Tuition: _____

- Out-of-state Tuition: _____
- Public or Private: _____
- Application due: _____

3. Student Body

Total enrollment: _____

Racial-ethnic background
American Indian/Alaskan Native _____
Asian _____   Black _____
Hispanic _____

Multiracial _____   White _____
Native Hawaiian/Pacific Islander
_____

Out-of-state students _____
International students _____

4. Costs

In-state tuition _____
Out-of-state tuition _____
Fees _____

Books and Supplies _____
Room and board _____
Board and Transportation _____

5. Financial Aid

Forms: _____
Deadline: _____
Typical financial aid package:
_____

Financial aid Programs:
- _____
- _____
- _____

6. Admissions

Entrance difficulty for incoming students _____
Education required for admission _____
Application Requirements: High school GPA _____
Recommended Exams _____
Average SAT score: Reading _____ Math _____
ACT Average score: _____

College Research Project (cont.)

7. Academics	Degrees offered: _____ _____ _____ _____
8. Student Life	Student activities: • _____ • _____ • _____ • _____
9. Housing	Percentage of students who live on campus _____ Does school own or operates housing: _____ Highest year required to live on campus _____ Housing options _____
10. Student Services	Academic services for all students _____ _____ _____ Health and Legal services _____ _____ _____
11. Career Services	Percentage of graduates who had jobs within 6 months _____ Career Services Offered _____ _____ _____

Adapted from https://portal.azcis.intocareers.org/

Which Postsecondary Track may be right for you?

If you need help with choosing what type of postsecondary track is right for you, answer the four questions below. The letter you chose the most aligns with how you prefer to learn. Check the bottom of the page for the postsecondary school that could most closely align with your learning preferences.

How do you prefer to learn the basics

A. Listening to a teacher, reading about a subject, and possibly hands-on application once I'm knowledgeable about the subject.
B. Small classes that combine listening to a teacher and bookwork.
C. Small classes that combine listening to an instructor, watching an instructor perform an example, book work, and hands-on training.
D. Instruction combined with watching an example and then hands-on work.

Which would you rather do?

A. Get involved in a campus community (Greek, Sports, Clubs).
B. Gain professional knowledge that can be used to provide paid professional consulting to my community.
C. Gain a set of skills in a particular field in a relatively short period of time and use them later on to provide a paid service to my community.
D. Gain a set of specialized skills tailored to an employer's needs and get paid in the process.

How much variety would you like?

A. Education includes a variety of topics and subjects.
B. A framework of information that I could directly put to use.
C. Some variety in my education but focused on hands-on skills.
D. Focus on one field and acquire a set of specialized skills in that particular field.

Which interests you the most?

A. Researching, analyzing, and synthesizing information to become highly knowledgeable about the world and my field.
B. Combining research with pertinent information from a teacher to gain understanding about a topic that will directly benefit me or my community.
C. Learning a set of skills through hands-on that lead directly to a specific job/career.
D. Starting a job with progressive wage increases as my knowledge and skill levels increase.

Which letter did you select the most?

A. **Four-Year Colleges & Universities** offer a broad array of bachelor's degrees, also called the baccalaureate Bachelor of Arts or Bachelor of Science. Many also offer vocational certificates, associate, and master's degrees.

B. **Community Colleges** usually serve city, borough, or region residents. They typically offer vocational certificates and associate degrees and have minimal entrance requirements.

C. **Vocational Schools & Colleges** offer career and technical training in a hands-on environment near your community.

D. **Apprenticeships / Workforce** start you working from day one with on-the-job training and technical instruction. It can take one to six years for individuals to receive an industry-recognized credential that certifies occupational proficiency.

Adapted from: https://in.nau.edu/gear-up/senior-guide/

Postsecondary Education Pathway

Here are examples of postsecondary education pathways that offer different types of degrees.

Career Examples	Teacher, Architect, Marketing Manager, Engineer, Registered Nurse, Journalist, Computer Programmer, Software Developer	Web Developers, Mechanical/ Industrial Engineering Tech, Occupational Therapy Assistant, Air Traffic Controller, Paralegal	Carpenter, Plumber, Machine Operator, Construction Worker, Dog Trainer	Dental Assistant, Motorcycle Mechanic, Electrician, HVAC Tech, Masseuse, Welder, Cosmetologist	Lawyer, Doctor, Veterinarian, Dentist, Orthodontist, Pharmacist	Military Service
Degree or Credential	Bachelor's Degrees, Master's Degrees, Doctoral Degrees, Professional Degrees	Associate's degrees	No Degree, On-The-Job Training	Certificate	Professional Degrees (MD, DDS, JD)	Varies Enlisted Personnel: May Obtain a Trade Certificate, ROTC: Will Obtain a Bachelor's Degree Military Academy: Will Earn a Bachelor's Degree
Postsecondary Edition	Four-Year University or College	Community College	On-The-Job Training or Apprenticeship	Technical School	Professional School (E.g., Law School, Medical School, Dental School)	Military
Time to Complete Education/Training	4 years	2 years	Depends on Job: A Few Months to a Few Years	A few months – 1 year	2-8 years after a bachelor's degree	Training and Service Commitment Varies
Admission Requirements for Postsecondary Institution/Path	High School Diploma Sweet 16 Courses Academic Readiness Some Require ACT or SAT	High School Diploma	Most Require a High School Diploma, Some Do Not	High School Diploma	Must Complete a bachelor's degree First	High School Diploma to Enlist College Requirements For ROTC, and Additional Requirements for Military Academies.
Examples of Schools in Arizona that offer education needed	Northern Arizona University The University of Arizona Arizona State University	Arizona Western Coll Central Arizona College Cochise College Pima Community College, Mohave Community College Northland Pioneer Coll	Workplaces	Universal Technical Institute (UTI), Arizona School of Dental Assisting, Pima Medical Institute	Law School – ASU, Physical Therapy Program – NAU, Medical School – U of A, Veterinary School – Midwestern University	Army, Navy, Air Force, Marines, Coast Guard, ROTC programs at colleges in AZ, (No Military Academies are in AZ)

Adapted from: https://in.nau.edu/gear-up/senior-guide/

24

Historically Black Colleges and Universities (HBCUs)

There are 107 colleges in the United States that are identified by the US Department of Education as Historically Black Colleges and Universities (HBCUs). *http://www.thehundred-seven.org/hbculist.html*

Alabama
Alabama A&M University- Huntsville
Alabama State Univ- Montgomery
Bishop State Comm College - Mobile
Gadsden State College- Gadsden
J.F. Drake State Tech College- Huntsville
Lawson State Comm College- Birmingham
Miles College- Fairfield
Oakwood University- Huntsville
Selma University- Selma
Shelton State Comm College- Tuscaloosa
Stillman College- Tuscaloosa
Talladega College- Talladega
Tuskegee University- Tuskegee
H.Council Trenholm State Community College- Montgomery

Arkansas
University of Arkansas at Pine Bluff
Arkansas Baptist College- Little Rock
Philander Smith College- Little Rock
Shorter College- North Little Rock

Delaware
Delaware State University- Dover

District of Columbia
University of the District of Columbia
Howard University

Florida
Bethune Cookman Univ- Daytona Beach
Edward Waters University- Jacksonville
Florida A&M University- Tallahassee
Florida Memorial Univ- Miami Gardens

Georgia
Albany State University- Albany
Clark Atlanta University- Atlanta
Fort Valley State University- Fort Valley
Interdenominational Theo Center- Atlanta
Morehouse College- Atlanta
Morehouse School of Medicine- Atlanta
Morris Brown College- Atlanta
Paine College- Augusta
Savannah State University- Savannah
Spelman College- Atlanta

Kentucky
Kentucky State University- Frankfort
Simmons College of Kentucky- Louisville

Louisiana
Dillard University-New Orleans
Grambling State University- Grambling
Southern Univ A&M College- Baton Rouge
Southern Univ New Orleans- New Orleans
Southern University-Shreveport
Xavier University- New Orleans

Maryland
Bowie State University- Bowie
Coppin State University- Baltimore
University of Maryland- Eastern Shore- Princess Anne
Morgan State University- Baltimore

Mississippi
Alcorn State University- Lorman
Coahoma Community College- Clarksdale
Hinds County Community College- Utica
Jackson State University- Jackson
Mississippi Valley State Univ- Itta Bena
Rust College- Holly Springs
Tougaloo College- Tougaloo

Missouri
Harris-Stowe State University- St. Louis
Lincoln University- Jefferson City

North Carolina
Bennett College- Greensboro
Elizabeth City State Univ- Elizabeth City
Fayetteville State University- Fayetteville
Johnson C. Smith University- Charlotte
Livingstone College- Salisbury
North Carolina Central University- Durham
North Carolina A&T State University- Greensboro
Shaw University- Raleigh
St. Augustine's University- Raleigh
Winston-Salem State Univ- Winston Salem

Ohio
Central State University- Wilberforce
Wilberforce University- Wilberforce

Oklahoma
Langston University- Langston

Pennsylvania
Cheyney University- Cheyney
The Lincoln University- Lincoln University

South Carolina
Allen University- Columbia
Benedict College- Columbia
Claflin University- Orangeburg
Clinton College- Rock Hill
Denmark Technical College- Denmark
Morris College- Sumter
South Carolina State Univ- Orangeburg
Voorhees University- Denmark

Tennessee
American Baptist University- Nashville
Fisk University- Nashville
Lane College- Jackson
LeMoyne Owen College- Memphis
Tennessee
Meharry Medical College
Tennessee State University- Nashville

Texas
Huston-Tillotson University-Austin
Jarvis Christian College- Hawkins
Paul Quinn College- Dallas
Prairie View A&M University- Prairie View
Southwestern Christian College- Terrell
St. Philip's College- San Antonio
Texas College- Tyler
Texas Southern University- Houston
Wiley College- Marshall

US Virgin Islands
University of the Virgin Islands- St. Thomas & St. Croix

Virginia
Hampton University- Hampton
Norfolk State University- Norfolk
Virginia State University- Petersburg
Virginia Union University- Richmond
Virginia Univ of Lynchburg- Lynchburg

West Virginia
Bluefield State College- Bluefield
West Virginia State University- Institute

College Application Platforms

COMMON APP
1000+ colleges

https://www.commonapp.org/ (the most widely used college application system today, serving approximately 900 colleges and universities worldwide, including all Ivy League schools and many top public and private schools)

COALITION APP
90+ colleges

https://www.coalitionforcollegeaccess.org/ (a group of approximately 90 U.S. higher education institutions dedicated to supporting all students, especially those from underrepresented groups, throughout the college application process)

COMMON BLACK COLLEGE APP
68 HBCUs

https://commonblackcollegeapp.com/ (prospective students can apply to 68 Historically Black Colleges and Universities for a single $20 fee using the Common Black College App)

INDIVIDUAL COLLEGE WEBSITE ONLINE APPLICATION

This is a separate online application that is created and maintained by the school itself and only applies to a specific school.

QUEST BRIDGE

https://www.questbridge.org/ (primarily functions as a scholarship-matching service)

UNIVERSAL APP

https://www.universalcollegeapp.com/ (this general application is used by far fewer schools and partner with approximately two member institutions)

PAPER APPLICATION: This is a paper version of the school's specific application.

Military

A military recruiter can help answer questions about service, providing a positive but realistic assessment of opportunities. A recruiter looks for qualified candidates for their respective branch and provides information regarding military benefits. Your high school counselor can give you dates of when recruiters will visit your school.

ASVAB

The Armed Services Vocational Aptitude Battery (ASVAB) is a multiple-choice test that determines enlistment qualification. Just like any other test, you should prepare for the ASVAB. Learn more about the ASVAB and how to prepare by visiting the sites below:

For general information:	For online ASVAB test prep:
• https://www.officialasvab.com/	• https://www.march2success.com/ • https://asvabtutor.com/ • https://www.asvabpracticetests.com/

Can You Use Your IEP in College?

By Samantha Fecich, Ph.D. and Mackenzie Caporale
https://www.bestcolleges.com/blog/iep-college/

Laws such as the Americans with Disabilities Act {ADA) and the Individuals with Disabilities Education Act {IDEA) are there to protect students' rights and ensure access to accommodations. However, expecting that a student's IEP will seamlessly follow them to college is a common misunderstanding.

Can You Use Your IEP Accommodations in College?

No, there is no special education placement or IEP in college. However, while the IEP process only applies to students until high school graduation, other laws protect the rights of disabled college students and their accommodations — and their IEP can be used as a starting point in obtaining those accommodations.

Section 504 of the Rehabilitation Act and the Americans With Disabilities Act {ADA) require colleges to provide accommodations for students with disabilities. The difference between these laws is that IDEA is a special education law. In contrast, Section 504 and ADA are civil rights laws.

The purpose of Section 504 is to provide services to enable students to learn alongside their peers. The primary difference in how Section 504 is utilized on a college campus is by who starts the process. In college, the student must self-disclose and request accommodations.

How to Get Disability Accommodations in College

To request disability accommodations in college, you must first meet with the disability services coordinator at your school. This should be done as soon as you commit to your college to ensure you have ample time to get any extra paperwork the disabilities services office may need. Review your IEP and create a list of your requested accommodations. Reflect on what accommodations were imperative to your achievements and identify any unused accommodations.

Most Common Accommodations in College

Additional Time on Exams: Sometimes, students are given time and a half to complete a test. For example, for a test that generally takes one hour to complete, the student can take as long as 2.5 hours.

Different Testing Locations: This accommodation allows students to take an exam in a different learning environment, usually in a distraction-free space. Some colleges have testing centers specifically designed for this purpose.

Exam Readers: Special technology can read exam questions and prompts to you. For example, Microsoft's Immersive Reader can read the text aloud, highlight it as it reads, and provide a picture dictionary.

Enlarged Print: Instead of using a 12- or 14-point font on an exam, assignment, or worksheet, you can ask for a larger font to make it easier to read.

Extra White Space on Exams: When given an exam, you can ask for extra space — so instead of having 10 problems on a page, you have two pages with five problems each. The white space can be useful for jotting down ideas, solving a problem, or working out an equation.

Preferred Seating: Sitting near the front or near the door during class to facilitate your learning is a common option for college students.

Note Taker: This accommodation allows someone to take notes for you during class. For example, if you have limited use of your hands, you can request a note-taker for your courses.

Digital Textbooks and Workbooks: Having a digital version of a textbook or workbook allows you to highlight, add notes, read aloud text to speech, zoom in, and use other digital accommodations. Some textbooks also have online portals that link to additional content, videos, and audio portions of the book.

Preparation Materials: This accommodation allows students to access presentations or lecture content beforehand. This can be useful for students who need it to be prepared on a screen or e-reader or for students who may need visual aids to be able to absorb lecture material.

Track College Applications

As you begin the college application process, apply to a variety of colleges, including a safe choice, a realistic choice, and a reach.

- **Safe choice:** Your academic credentials fall above the school's range for the average freshman. It's safe to anticipate acceptance.
- **Realistic choice:** Your academic credentials fall within (or even exceed) the school's range for the average freshman. There are no guarantees, but it's reasonable to expect acceptance.
- **Reach choice:** Your academic credentials fall below admission guidelines, but it's important to reach for the stars. Go for it and apply to that selective dream school.

Use this table to keep track of your progress on your college applications:

	College Name/Website	Date you applied	Date you sent application	Date sent official HS transcript	Date you sent test scores: CLEP, AP, ACT, SAT	Acceptance Yes or No	Financial award letter Yes or No
1.							
2.							
3.							
4.							
5.							
6.							

Common App Essays Prompts 2023-2024

https://www.vappingo.com/word-blog/common-app-essays-prompts-2023-2024/

1	Share a significant aspect of your identity	A personal narrative that showcases a unique aspect of the applicant	Avoid cliches and superficial descriptions. Be introspective and reflective.
2	Describe a challenge and how you overcame it	An essay that shows how the applicant handled adversity and grew from the experience	Avoid presenting yourself as a victim or blaming others for your setbacks. Focus on your growth and development.
3	Discuss a time when you challenged an idea or belief	An essay that demonstrates critical thinking and intellectual curiosity	Avoid controversial or offensive topics that could alienate your reader. Be respectful and open-minded.
4	Reflect on a moment of gratitude	A personal narrative that shows how someone else's actions impacted you	Avoid being too general or cliched. Be specific and thoughtful.
5	Describe a personal growth experience	An essay that showcases how the applicant learned about themselves or others	Avoid bragging or presenting yourself as perfect. Be honest about your flaws and challenges.
6	Discuss an intellectual passion	An essay that reveals the applicant's interests and curiosity	Avoid being too obscure or abstract. Make sure your passion is something you can explain in detail.
7	Share an essay on any topic	An opportunity for the applicant to showcase their writing and creativity	Avoid cliches or writing on a topic that does not showcase your unique voice and perspective. Be thoughtful and original.

Common App Essays (example)

https://www.scribd.com/document/669563062/CollegeAdvisor-60FreeEssayExamples-EBook

Some students have a background, identity, interest, or talent that is so meaningful they believe their application would be incomplete without it. If this sounds like you, then please share your story.

All my life I have been drawn to ducks. Over the past 17 years, I have amassed a collection of over sixty rubber duckies, occupying three shelves of my closet, varying in sizes, colors, and designs, all pieces of their unique identities. When I glimpse the Queen Elizabeth duck in her purple dress or the Rock Star duck with his red mohawk, I can't help but wonder what kind of duck I would be.

During middle school, I'd have quickly responded: a computer duck! For several years, my singular focus was on robotics. This wasn't because computer science was my one true passion, but more because I felt pressure to answer widespread calls for "more women in STEM". As the lead coder on my team, I was proud when we excelled in the Robot Game at Legoland's Semi Regional Competition, and although my hard work paid off, I was dissatisfied. I enjoyed advocating for female representation in computer science at city council meetings and being asked to teach coding workshops for teachers, but I was not my whole self. I'd tried too hard to mold myself into the person I thought others expected me to be and in doing so, I lost touch with my other interests.

However, with the pandemic, I had the time and space to think about what I really valued and reconnect to my inner voice. I began to understand that being singularly focused on computer science was simply not me. I am passionate about swimming, politics, music, and mental health advocacy. Any rubber duckie that represents me needs to reflect all these pieces of me. My multifaceted duck would undoubtedly wear a pair of goggles—swimming has helped me build my tenacity. Through my years of swimming, I've learned that the only race that matters is my own: self-improvement is the real reward.

My duck would also wear a campaign t-shirt to represent my involvement in over 20 local, state, and national campaigns. Through all of the door-to-door outreach and the thousands of conversations while phone banking, I've learned to discuss uncomfortable, controversial topics with ease. I learned to listen first and speak second. Then, as I started my internship with Congresswoman Kim, I learned to shift the conversations I had with constituents. As an intern, there was a new gravity to my work. In helping to process Afghanistan refugee and Social Security casework, the quality and accuracy of my work were consequential. Previously, I had relied on adults for guidance, but now they depended on me. When people called to request emergency evacuation assistance or to track down their stimulus checks, I was the first voice they heard. Through the process, I developed a newfound confidence in my ability to give back to members of my community. My rubber ducky would also have a butterfly perched on her orange bill to represent the mental health awareness project I started with friends. It began as a way to share mental wellness strategies I'd developed during quarantine, but it grew into a platform where I could use my own struggles with burnout and anxiety to help others. Through this I learned I am not alone during difficult times and that being vulnerable is an asset I can use to advocate for issues I care about like suicide prevention.

Sure, there is value in "branding" oneself--picking one thing to specialize in--but I've learned that doing so puts me at the risk of losing touch with my whole self. Everyone has a dynamic personality and a set of interests that makes them unique, but I like to think that just like me, each duck has a life beyond its branded costume. I have many passions--swimming, politics, mental health--choosing just one would be a disservice to all the other parts of me. Ultimately, my goal is to waddle in my own authentic way.

Writing/Graphic Organizer
Introduction Paragraph

Prompt:		
Opinion/Position:		
Main Idea/Reason 1:	**Main Idea/Reason 2:**	**Main Idea/Reason 3:**
Details:	**Details:**	**Details:**

Attention Getter:
Background/Information/Issues sentences:
Thesis (your opinion – include 3 reasons):

Body 1: Reason 1 (topic sentence with transition words)

Details/Support (complete sentences)

1.

2.

3.

4.

Writing/Graphic Organizer (cont.)

Body 2: Reason 2 (topic sentence with transition words)

> [blank box]

Details/Support (complete sentences)

1.
2.
3.
4.

Body 3: Reason 3 (topic sentence with transition words)

> [blank box]

Details/Support (complete sentences)

1.
2.
3.
4.

Conclusion Paragraph

Rewrite Thesis (include 3 reasons):

Sum up/Wrap-up/Recommendation:

College Essay Rubric

CRITERIA	EXCELLENT	GOOD	SATISFACTORY	MINIMUM
FORMAT	•Typed/computer generated • Clean and neat • Multi-paragraph essay format • Professional font: 12-point; Times New Roman	• Typed/computer generated • Multi-paragraph essay format • Professional font: 12-point; Times New Roman	• Typed/computer generated • Multi-paragraph essay format • Inappropriate font or point size	•Typed/computer generated faint or smudged • Multi-paragraph essay format not-used • Inappropriate font or point size
Ranking Points	10	8	7	6
CONTENT INTRODUCTION	• Introduction captures the reader's attention • Intro begins with a quotation, a challenge, a reflection, or an idea or inspiration	• Introduction attempts to capture the reader's attention • Intro begins with a quotation, a challenge, a reflection, or an idea or inspiration	• Introduction begins with a question or does not inspire the reader	• No recognizable introduction or is muddled • Intro does not relate to the writing prompt
Ranking Points	10	a	7	5-o
CONTENT - MAIN BODY	• Body focuses on student's past, present, and future • Body directly relates to writing prompt • Essay is 250 - 600 words* • No or very few repeated or unnecessary words	• Body focuses on student's past, present, and future • Body directly relates to writing prompt • Essay is 250 - 600 words* • A few repeated or unnecessary words	• Body includes student's past, present, and future • Body sometimes relates to writing prompt • Essay is 250 - 600 words* • Some repeated or unnecessary words	• Body includes some of student's past, present, and future • Body rarely relates to writing prompt • Essay is not 250 - 600 words* • Many repeated or unnecessary words
Ranking Points	10	8	7	5-0
CONTENT- CLOSING	• Conclusion is very personal and ties in with introduction • Leaves the reader with a strong idea of who the writer is • Conveys a positive and clear vision for the future	•Conclusion is personal and ties in with introduction • Leaves the reader with an idea of who the writer is • Conveys a positive vision for the future	• Conclusion is personal and ties in with introduction • Leaves the reader with somewhat of an idea of who the writer is	• Conclusion is not particularly personal and doesn't tie in with introduction • Leaves the reader with a vague idea of who the writer is
Ranking Points	10	8	7	5-0
SPELLING & GRAMMAR	No spelling errors No grammar errors	1-2 spelling errors 1-2 grammar errors	3-4 spelling errors 3-4 grammar errors	5-6 spelling errors 5-6 grammar errors
Ranking Points	10	8	7	5-0

Letter of Recommendation Tips

Consider these helpful tips to assist you in asking for letters of recommendation.

1. It is a good idea to ask a variety of people (ex. boss, volunteer coordinator, teacher, counselor, coach, club sponsor). Ask each person to highlight different attributes. Consider having recommenders who can:

• reflect on your intellectual growth • be able to tell a good story about you • describe who you are outside the classroom • provide specific attributes about you	• assess your academic and personal achievements and potential • know you well enough to evaluate your relevant qualifications

2. Plan to submit your application before the actual deadline. Giving yourself an early deadline allows you to prepare all of the required documents with ample time and helps minimize last-minute stress. Your deadline should be at least 2 weeks prior.

3. It is important that you make your request for a letter of recommendation early. Preferably, ask your recommender 1 month in advance but with at least a minimum of 2 full weeks to prepare your letter. List YOUR deadline (the date you prepared above) as the date needed on your request form. Once again, this will allow you to submit your documents ahead of time.

4. Giving your recommenders a bit of guidance on what they should express about you in the letter will only make their job easier. Fill out the student self-assessment and tailor the answers about yourself a little different for each recommender. This will allow each recommender to target different qualities about you and avoid repeating the same areas.

5. Provide your recommender with an organized folder that includes:
   - Your request form and self-assessment
   - A list of all the scholarships/colleges that need recommendations
   - Any required forms for those applications
   - Resume, transcripts, personal statement (as applicable)

6. Double check the letter of recommendation guidelines for each application

7. Send a "Thank You" note to your recommender.

Letter of Recommendation Request Form

Recommender Name: _____

Student Name: _____

Date Requested: _____

Date Needed: _____

Name/Address of Scholarship/College to be listed on letter:

_____

_____

Process for submitting letter of recommendation:

- ☐ return to student
- ☐ mail to address stated above
- ☐ submit online
- ☐ other:

Scholarship/College Application Criteria:

_____

_____

Student's Prospective College Major/Program:

_____

_____

Student should attach if available/applicable:

- Resume
- Transcripts
- Personal statement/essay
- A copy of the scholarship application or link to the application

Letter of Recommendation

Student Self-Assessment for Recommender

1. What do you hope to accomplish in college and after? Consider your career goals and your broader goals.

   _____

   _____

   _____

2. Academic accomplishments (AP, Honors, AVID, IB, etc.,) or activities you are proud of, the amount of time spent, and explain why you take pride in it. List leadership positions you held.

   _____

   _____

3. What are your activities outside of school? Highlight leadership or volunteer work, positions held in community. Include years and the amount of time you dedicated to activities.

   _____

   _____

4. List awards and honors. _____

   _____

5. List three distinguishing or admirable qualities. Explain each.

   _____

   _____

6. Explain why you need financial assistance.

   _____

   _____

7. What are obstacles you have overcome.

   _____

   _____

Create a Resume

Content and format are equally important. If your work history is strong, but the format is difficult to read or contains typos, employers won't consider you. The example on the following page is clear, easy to read, and error-free.

Resume basics

1. **Heading:** Include your name, address, email address, and phone number. Make it stand out and make an impression by using large, bold font. Make sure your email is professional (not starwarsfan@hotmail.com or crzychik@aol.com, for example).

2. **Education:** As a high school student, include your GPA if it is 3.0 or above. List courses that reflect your work ethic and high aspirations, such as AP or dual enrollment courses, and relevant coursework for the job you're applying to. After college graduation, don't include high school information.

3. **Experience or Major Achievements:** Include your job title, the employer, the location (city and state, at minimum), and the dates of employment for each job listed. Include a brief description of your achievements / responsibilities. Ideally, paid work and unpaid work (community service) are listed separately.

4. **Honors / Awards / Scholarships:** Include the name of the organization that bestowed the honor / award and the date. Only include scholarships based on merit, not financial need.

5. **Special Skills / Highlights:** List any unique, relevant, or necessary skills not reflected in education or experience (e.g., foreign language fluency, computer program expertise, etc.).

6. **References:** Ask permission first to list people as a reference and provide them with a copy of your resume

Jane Doe

Scottsdale, AZ, 852571 480-867-5309 I professionalemail@gmail.com

Organized and creative student who has completed two years of Software Development course content. Skilled in Java and C # programming languages.

Education

Hogwarts Academy, Phoenix, AZ | Expected Graduation 2021

GPA: 3.6

Certifications:

2020

- Microsoft Technology Associate
- Software Development Program- Introduction to Software Development, AP English

Skills and Proficiencies

- Java (Beginner)
- C # (Proficient)
- Fluent in English and Spanish

Experience

Krusty Krab, Mesa, AZ | 06/2020 – Current

- Manage 200 reservations, cancellations and inquires on a weekly basis to help business engagement
- Greet and escort 150 patrons to their tables and present menus in a friendly manner to encourage customer satisfaction
- Assisted management by communicating customer complaints to appropriate teams and resolving issues in a timely manner

Volunteer Work

Arizona Humane Society, Mesa, AZ | 07/2021 – Current

Volunteer

- Facilitated daily walks for over 100 dogs to prevent injuries and hazards from cage confinement
- Performed daily maintenance to keep animals' food, water, and cages fresh
- Assisted in paperwork preparation to improve speed and accuracy in adoption process

Extracurriculars or Leadership Experience

Softball Captain | 07/2020 – 10/2020

- Executed daily warmups to prevent team injuries
- Promoted team spirit by creating team building activities for teammates to participate in

Awards or Achievements

- Volunteer of the Year, Arizona Humane Society (2020)

Pre-FAFSA Information

Fill out the following information to keep everything in one place. You'll need it to create your FSA ID and to complete the FAFSA.

1. Your email **(not your high school email)**: _____ cell phone: _____

    Parent email: _____ cell phone: _____

2. Are you an Arizona resident? ☐ Yes ☐ No

    If no, the month / year you moved to Arizona. _____

3. Are your parents Arizona residents? ☐ Yes ☐ No

    If no, the month / year your parents moved to Arizona. _____

4. Your Social Security number-------------------------------------- _____

5. Your parents' Social Security numbers (if your parent doesn't have a Social Security Number, use all 0's):

    Parent 1: _____ - _____ - _____   Parent 2 -------------------------------- _____

6. If you are not a U. S. citizen, what is your permanent resident card A #: _____

7. What are your parents' dates of birth? Parent 1 D.O.B. _____ Parent 2 D.O.B. _____

8. Do you have a driver's license? ☐ Yes ☐ No

9. Your driver's license #: _____ Expiration date:_____

10. What is the month and year your parents were married, divorced, or separated? _____

11. What is the highest level of school your parents completed? (Circle one for each parent).

    Parent 1: Middle School / Jr. High   High School   College or beyond   Other / unknown

    Parent 2: Middle School / Jr. High   High School   College or beyond   Other / unknown

https://studentaid.gov/h/apply-for-aid/fafsa

At https://studentaid.gov/h/apply-for-aid/fafsa, you can complete, submit, and track your application. If you do not have internet access, you can get a paper copy by calling 1-800-4-FED-AID (433-3243). Remember, filing the FAFSA is free. If you see a website or ad requesting a fee, steer clear!

You can also complete the FAFSA form using the myStudentAid app. Download the myStudentAid app in the Apple App Store (iOS) or Google Play (Android).

Adapted from: https://in.nau.edu/gear-up/senior-guide/

Financial Aid Checklist for FAFSA/CSS Profile

- Create a folder to store financial aid documents
- Name it: Financial Aid I YEAR I Student Initials
- Gather Important Documents and upload them into the folder
- Social Security numbers for student and both parents
- Student Driver's License (if applicable)
- Alien registration or permanent resident cards if you or your parents are not U.S. citizens
- W2s for Parents
- W2s for the student (if applicable)
- Tax Returns for Parents
- Tax Returns for the student (if applicable)
- Business Tax Returns (if applicable)
- Current bank statements
- An estimate of money expected to earn in the current year for both parents
- Parents' DOB and Date of Marriage (if applicable), and Date of Divorce (if applicable)
- Financial information on savings, investments (401Ks, stocks), and business assets for Parents and Students (529 Plans)
- Housing and Real Estate information: purchase date, the purchase price
- Current value
- Medical or Dental bills (if significant)
- Any other financial information that tells the family's financial story
- Obtain the College Board Username and PW
- The cost to file the CSS Profile form is $25 plus $16 to submit the application to an additional school payable directly to the College Board website.
- Get an FSA I.D -- Student AND Parent
- Go to https://fsaid.ed.gov
- The student and one of the parents will need to sign up for a Federal Student Aid ID, also called an FSA ID for us to work on the FAFSA form and sign it electronically.
- The website will walk you through a quick and easy login process.
- FAFSA – www.fafsa.gov or www.fafsa.ed.gov
- CSS Profile – www.cssprofile.org

Finding Scholarships & The Scholarship Log

Scholarships are a form of financial aid that is awarded to students for outstanding academics, community service, extra-curricular activities, sports or other skills they possess. The scholarship application should be completed in a timely fashion, directions should be followed exactly, and all requested materials must be submitted to the awarding organization by the specified deadline.

Scholarship opportunities can be found at the following:

• Employers	• Military and Veteran Organizations	• Religious Org.
• Local stores	• Unions High Schools	• Library
• Volunteer organizations	• PSAT {National Merit}	• Internet Search Sites
• Organizations and Clubs		• Newspaper

10 Common Scholarship Essay Questions

- Tell Us About Yourself
- How Will This Scholarship Make a Difference for You?
- Can You Tell Us About a Time You Failed? What Did You Learn from That Experience?
- Tell Us About a Contribution You've Made to Your Community
- What Are Your Academic {or Professional} Goals?
- Tell Us About a Time Where You Stepped Up as a Leader
- Who Has Been Your Biggest Influence {or Inspiration)?
- Why Do You Want to Go to College?
- How Are You Planning on Financing Your College Education?
- Why Do You Deserve This Scholarship?
  https://thescholarshipsystem.com/blog-for-students-families/10-common-scholarship-essay-questions-and-how-to-answer-them/

Essay Dos and Don'ts:

Dos: Make sure to do these!		Don'ts: Don't make these mistakes	
Answer the question	Strong intro. & conclusion	Essay too short or too long	Include irrelevant info.
Proofread for errors	Portray your personality	List your accomplishments	No structure/flow
List strong goals within reach	Be professional	Use cliches	Essay not typed
Use examples/stories	Be positive! Avoid negativity	Spelling/grammar errors	Crazy font or format

Scholarship Search Sites & Links

- ADAIR/ACE: http://www.adairfamilyfoundation.org/
- Alpha Kappa Alpha Sorority, Inc. - DBO {Phoenix}: https://f4c1059b-6fdc-462d-9331-e96dcfe20dc2.filesusr.com/ugd/dcd084_148ebff203254a5e8b824429f73fca11.pdf
- American Indian College Fund- www.collegefund.org
- Arizona Community Foundation Scholarship: http://www.azfoundation.org/scholarships/scholarshipopportunities.aspx
- Arizona Community Foundation: https://www.azfoundation.org/Scholarships/Scholarship-Opportunities
- Arizona Grants: http://www.azgrants.gov/
- Arizona Public Service {APS}: https://www.aps.com/en/About/Community/In-the-Community/Education/Scholarships

Scholarship Search Sites & Links (cont.)

- Arizona State University Legacy: https://scholarships.asu.edu/scholarship/96233
- AXA Foundation: https://www.scholarships.com/axa-achievement-scholarship/
- Baird Scholarship - University of AZ: https://honors.arizona.edu/baird-scholarship
- Big Sun Athletic Organization: https://bigsunathletics.com/
- Bryan Cameron Foundation: https://www.bryancameroneducationfoundation.org/cameron-impact-scholarship
- Burger King: https://bkmclamorefoundation.org/who-we-are/programs/burger-king-scholars-program/
- CIA Undergraduate Scholars: https://www.cia.gov/careers/student-opportunities/undergraduate-scholarship-program.html
- Coca Cola: https://www.coca-colascholarsfoundation.org/apply/
- College Depot Scholarships: http://www.phoenixpubliclibrary.org/collegedepot/Pages/Scholarships.aspx
- CVS Health Scholarship Program: https://cvshealth.com/social-responsibility/our-giving/cvs-health-foundation
- Delta Sigma Theta - Phoenix Metro: https://www.dstphoenixalumnae.org/programs/educationaldevelopment/scholarship/
- Delta Sigma Theta - Tempe: https://dsttempe.org/educational-development
- Dorrance Merit ACF: http://www.dorrancescholarship.org/
- Dorrance Scholarship Programs: https://dorrancescholarship.org/
- Fast Web: www.fastweb.com
- FinAid: www.finaid.org/age13
- FLINN Foundation: https://flinn.org/flinn-scholars/the-scholarship/apply/
- Gates Scholarship: https://www.thegatesscholarship.org/scholarship
- Hispanic Scholarship Fund- www.latinocollegedollars.org
- http://www.usnews.com/scholarshipcoach
- Jack Kent Cooke: https://www.jkcf.org/our-scholarships/
- Jackie Robinson Foundation: https://www.jackierobinson.org/apply/
- Jacques Avent: https://azfoundation.academicworks.com/opportunities/4237
- JLV College Counseling Scholarships: https://jlvcollegecounseling.com/scholarships/
- Laveen Community Council: https://www.laveen.org/scholarship.html
- Louis Stokes Health Scholars: https://cbcfinc.academicworks.com/opportunities/635
- Maricopa Community Colleges Foundation: https://mcccd.scholarships.ngwebsolutions.com/CMXAdmin/Cmx_Content.aspx?cpId=1395
- Maricopa Community Colleges Scholarships: https://maricopa.academicworks.com/
- Medical needs offers- www.needymeds.com/scholarships.taf
- National Honor Society: https://www.nhs.us/students/the-nhs-scholarship/
- Obama Scholarship: https://students.asu.edu/obama
- OR https://dboforms.wufoo.com/forms/20192020-scholarship-application/
- Paul Quinn: https://www.unigo.com/scholarships/by-college/paul-quinn-college-scholarships
- Phoenix Union Foundation: https://www.foundation4education.org/what-we-do/scholarships/
- PXU Black Alliance Scholarships: https://forms.office.com/Pages/ResponsePage.aspx?id=YRiAyqiKVU6gPHPtFl268i9lgZ9MqoVLh2KBKS6IijhUN1VTVTYyVkcyUjJEUEs2TUM5SFJTUVFSSy4u

Scholarship Search Sites & Links (cont.)

- Phoenix Suns Charities: https://www.nba.com/suns/phoenix-suns-charities-sunsstudent-scholarship-applications-now-available#
- Quest Bridge: https://www.questbridge.org/high-school-students
- Raise Me: www.raise.me
- Ron Brown Scholar: https://www.ronbrown.org/section/apply/eligibility-requirements
- Ronald McDonald Charities: https://worldscholarshipforum.com/rmhc-scholarship/#12-3--rmhc-african-american-future-achievers-
- Sallie Mae Scholarships: https://www.salliemae.com/college-planning/college-scholarships/
- Scholarships 360: https://scholarships360.org/
- Scholarships a-z: https://scholarshipsaz.org/
- Scholarships: https://www.scholarships.com/
- Sphinx Educational Fund: http://www.sphinxeducationalfund.org/scholarship.html
- Tom Joyner College Fund {TMCF}: https://tomjoynerfoundation.org/scholarships/
- Unigo Scholarships: http://www.unigo.com/
- United Negro College Fund - www.blackstudents.blacknews.org
- United Negro College Fund {UNCF}: https://uncf.org/scholarships
- Walmart Dependent Scholarships: https://programs.applyists.com/walmartdependent/
- Wendy's Heisman Scholarship: https://heismanscholarship.com/application/
- William Randolph Hearst: https://www.hearstfdn.org/
- www.aallnet.org
- www.azcisintocareers.org {education tab- AZ scholarships}
- www.bigfuture.collegeboard.org
- www.cappex.com
- www.careerinfonet.org/scholarshipsearch
- www.collegeexpress.com
- www.gocollege.com
- www.goingmerry.com
- www.internationalscholarships.com {foreign study}
- www.myscholly.com
- www.naas.org
- www.niche.com
- www.rmhc.org
- www.scholarshipamerica.org
- www.scholarshipguidance.com
- www.scholarshipowl.com
- www.scholarshippoints.com
- www.scholarships.com
- www.scholly.com
- www.studentaid.ed.gov
- www.studentscholarships.org
- www.supercollege.com
- www.thesimpledollar.com/college-scholarship-guide

Colleges That Cover 100% of Financial Need

The following colleges have a stated commitment to provide all admitted US citizens and US permanent residents with a financial aid package that covers 100% of their financial needs.

Amherst College	www.amherst.edu/admission/financial_aid
Bowdoin College	www.bowdoin.edu/student-aid/index.html
Brown University	www.brown.edu/about/administration/financial-aid/financial-aid-basics
Colby College	www.colby.edu/admission/apply/#financial-aid
Columbia University	cc-seas.financialaid.columbia.edu/how/aid/works
Grinnell College	www.grinnell.edu/admission/financial-aid
Harvard University	college.harvard.edu/financial-aid/how-aid-works
Johns Hopkins University	www.jhu.edu/admissions/financial-aid/
Massachusetts Institute of Technology MIT	sfs.mit.edu/undergraduate-students/the-cost-of-attendance/making-mit-affordable/
Pomona College	www.pomona.edu/financial-aid
Princeton University	admission.princeton.edu/cost-aid
Rice University	financialaid.rice.edu/rice-investment
Stanford University	admission.stanford.edu/afford/
Swarthmore College	www.swarthmore.edu/financial-aid
University of Chicago	collegeadmissions.uchicago.edu/cost-aid
University of Pennsylvania	srfs.upenn.edu/financial-aid
Washington and Lee University	my.wlu.edu/financial-aid/types-of-aid/the-wandl-promise
Yale University	admissions.yale.edu/affordability-basics
Davidson College	www.davidson.edu/admission-and-financial-aid/financial-aid
Northwestern University	admissions.northwestern.edu/tuition-aid/
Vanderbilt University	www.vanderbilt.edu/financialaid/
Claremont McKenna College	www.cmc.edu/financial-aid/prospective-and-new-students
Colorado College	www.coloradocollege.edu/admission/financialaid/funding_guide/index.html
Cornell University	finaid.cornell.edu/types-aid
Denison University	denison.edu/campus/admission/applying-for-financial-aid
Emory University	apply.emory.edu/financial-aid/index.html
Franklin & Marshall College	www.fandm.edu/financial-aid/our-committment-to-need-based-aid
Georgetown University	finaid.georgetown.edu/financial-resources/undergrad-scholarships/
Hamilton College	www.hamilton.edu/admission/finaid
Lehigh University	wwwl.lehigh.edu/admissions/tuition-affording-college

Colleges That Cover 100% of Financial Need

Macalester College	www.macalester.edu/admissions/financial-aid/
Middlebury College	www.middlebury.edu/college/admissions/affordability
Minerva Schools at KGI	www.minerva.kgi.edu/undergraduate-program/tuition-aid/financial-aid/
Mount Holyoke College	www.mtholyoke.edu/admission/tuition_finaid
Oberlin College	www.oberlin.edu/financial-aid
Occidental College	www.oxy.edu/admission-aid/costs-financial-aid/how-financial-aid-works
Reed College	www.reed.edu/financialaid/index.html
Scripps College	www.scrippscollege.edu/financialaid/
Sewanee: The University of the South	new.sewanee.edu/admission-aid/meeting-full-need/
Soka University of America	www.soka.edu/financial-aid-tuition/aid-undergraduate-students/aid-domestic-undergraduates
Trinity College	www.trincoll.edu/admissions/finaid/
University of Notre Dame	financialaid.nd.edu/
University of Richmond	financialaid.richmond.edu/
University of Rochester	www.rochester.edu/financial-aid/prospective-undergraduates/
Aquinas College	aquinas.edu/marketing-and-communication/posts/aquinas-college-meet-full-demonstrated-financial-need-qualified
Boston College	www.bc.edu/bc-web/admission/affordability.html
Boston University	www.bu.edu/admissions/tuition-aid/scholarships-financial-aid/
California Institute of Technology	www.finaid.caltech.edu/HowItWorks
Carnegie Mellon University	admission.enrollment.cmu.edu/pages/applying-for-aid
College of the Holy Cross	www.holycross.edu/admissions-aid/financial-aid
Curtis Institute of Music	www.curtis.edu/admissions/financial-assistance/
Dickinson College	www.dickinson.edu/info/20081/financial_aid
Franklin W. Olin College of Engineering	www.olin.edu/admission/costs-financial-aid/
Harvey Mudd College	www.hmc.edu/admission/afford/
Kenyon College	www.kenyon.edu/admissions-aid/financial-aid-scholarships/
Northeastern University	studentfinance.northeastern.edu/applying-for-aid/undergraduate/the-northeastern-promise/
Pitzer College	www.pitzer.edu/financial-aid/
Skidmore College	www.skidmore.edu/admissions/aid/index.php
St. Olaf College	wp.stolaf.edu/admissions/afford/
Union College	www.union.edu/financial-aid-family-financing
University of Miami	admissions.miami.edu/undergraduate/financial-aid/index.html
University of North Carolina at Chapel Hill	admissions.unc.edu/afford/

Colleges That Cover 100% of Financial Need

University of Southern California	admission.usc.edu/learn/cost-financial-aid/
University of Virginia	sfs.virginia.edu/financial-aid-current-students/current-undergraduate-students/financial-aid-basics/determining-need
Wake Forest University	financialaid.wfu.edu/need-based-financial-aid/
United States Coast Guard Academy	uscga.edu/admissions/cost-and-tuition/
United States Merchant Marine Academy	www.usmma.edu/admissions/financial-aid
United States Military Academy	www.westpoint.edu/admissions
United States Naval Academy	www.usna.edu/Admissions/Student-Life/General-Information -for-Midshipmen.php
United States Air Force Academy	www.academyadmissions.com/why/education/

HISTORICALLY BLACK COLLEGES AND UNIVERSITIES (HBCU) SCHOLARSHIPS

Alabama A&M University	www.aamu.edu/admissions-aid/financial-aid/scholarships/index.html
Alabama State University	www.alasu.edu/admissions/undergrad-admissions/asu-academic-scholarships
Albany State University	www.asurams.edu/enrollment-management/financial-aid/financial-aid-scholarships
Alcorn State University	www.alcorn.edu/academics/schools-and-departments/school-of-education-and-psychology/scholarships/
Allen University	allenuniversity.edu/grants-and-scholarships
American Baptist College	abcnash.edu/admissions/financial-aid/
Arkansas Baptist College	arkansasbaptist.edu/scholarships-3/
Benedict College	benedict.edu/office-of-admissions-and-recruitment/office-of-financial-aid-and-
Bennett College	www.bennett.edu/admissions/financial-aid/scholarships/
Bethune-Cookman College	www.cookman.edu/aid/scholarships/index.html
Central State University	www.centralstate.edu/scholarship-central
Cheyney University	cheyney.edu/financialaid/grants-loans-scholarships/admissionsscholarships/
Claflin University	www.claflin.edu/admissions-aid/financial-aid/scholarships-and-grants
Clark Atlanta University	www.cau.edu/financialaid/scholarships-and-discounts.html
Clinton College	www.clintoncollege.edu/future-students/financial-aid
Coppin State University	www.coppin.edu/tuition-and-aid/scholarships-and-scholars-programs
Delaware State University	www.desu.edu/admissions/financial-aid/scholarships
Dillard University	mydu.dillard.edu/ICS/icsfs/2020-2021_Scholarship_Agreement.pdf?target=d1a614ff-c4c8-4dc4-8f52-cffac75483de
Edward Waters College	www.ewc.edu/wp-content/uploads/EWC-Scholarship-Application.pdf
Elizabeth City State University	www.ecsu.edu/financial-aid/index.php
Fayetteville State University	www.uncfsu.edu/paying-for-college/scholarships
Fisk University	www.fisk.edu/admissions/scholarships/
Florida Memorial University	apply.fmuniv.edu/portal/scholarships
Fort Valley State University	www.fvsu.edu/academics/scholarships
Grambling State University	gram.edu/finaid/scholarships/
Harris Stowe State University	go.hssu.edu/rspcontent_2021.html?wid=2&pid=15
Huston Tillotson State University	htu.edu/enrollment/financial-aid/scholarships-grants/
Jarvis Christian College	www.jarvis.edu/prospective-students/scholarships/
Jackson State University	sites.jsums.edu/scholarships/
Johnson Smith University	www.jcsu.edu/admissions/tuition-and-financial-aid/scholarships
Kentucky State University	www.kysu.edu/finance-and-administration/financial-aid/scholarships.php
Lane College	www.lanecollege.edu/financial-aid-tuition/scholarships
Lincoln University (MO)	www.lincolnu.edu/admissions/financial-aid/types-of-aid/scholarships1.html

47

HISTORICALLY BLACK COLLEGES AND UNIVERSITIES (HBCU) SCHOLARSHIPS

Lincoln University (PA)	www.lincoln.edu/admissions/undergraduate/scholarships/index.html
LeMoyne Owen College	www.loc.edu/enrollment-management/financial-aid/
Livingstone College	livingstone.edu/admission/
Mississippi Valley State University	www.mvsu.edu/prospective-students/scholarships
Miles College	www.miles.edu/sites/default/files/2021-12/ScholarshipApplication2020.pdf
Morgan State University	www.morgan.edu/finaid/scholarships
Morris College	www.morris.edu/financial-aid/financial-aid-at-a-glance-guide/scholarships
Norfolk State University	www.nsu.edu/financial-aid/scholarships
North Carolina Central University	www.nccu.edu/ssa
Paine College	www.paine.edu/web/admission/financial-aid/scholarships-honors-aawards
Paul Quinn College	paulquinn.edu/office-of-financial-aid/
Philander Smith University	www.philander.edu/admissions/types-of-aid/scholarships-and-grants/
Rust College	www.rustcollege.edu/prospective-students/financial-aid/scholarships/
Saint Augustine University	www.st-aug.edu/admissions/financial-aid/types-of-aid/scholarship/
Shaw University	www.shawu.edu/scholarships/
South Carolina State University	scsu.edu/registrars-office/life-scholarship-guidelines/
Southern University and A&M College	www.subr.edu/page/external-internal-scholarships
Southern University (NO)	www.suno.edu/page/financial-aid-scholarships
Stillman College	stillman.edu/financial-aid-office/scholarships/
Talladega College	www.talladega.edu/scholarships/
Tennessee State University	www.tnstate.edu/financial_aid/scholarships.aspx
Texas College	www.texascollege.edu/office-of-bradmissions/financial-aid/scholarships/
Tougaloo College	www.tougaloo.edu/admissions/scholarships
University of Arkansas Pine Bluff	www.uapb.edu/administration/enrollment_management/office_of_recruitment/scholarships.aspx
University of Maryland Eastern Shore	wwwcp.umes.edu/financialaid/scholarships/.
Virginia State University	www.vsu.edu/financial-aid/types-of-aid/scholarships.php
Virginia Union University	www.vuu.edu/financial-aid/scholarship-opportunities
Voorhees College	voorhees.edu/office-of-admissions/office-of-student-scholarships/
West Virginia State University	www.wvstateu.edu/admissions/scholarships.aspx
Wilberforce University	wilberforce.edu/scholarship-opportunity/
Wiley College	https://wileyc.edu/office-of-financial-aid

Scholarship Log

	Name of Scholarship / URL	Components (items needed to apply e.g., essay, recommendations, transcripts, applications, etc.	Value ($)	Deadline	Notes	Date received and amount of award
1.						
2.						
3.						
4.						
5.						
6.						
7.						
8.						
9.						
10						
11						

49

Accepted to College...
NOW WHAT?

1

GET MORE INFORMATION

ASK QUESTIONS

Make sure any questions you have about your school have been answered.

RESEARCH DEPARTMENTS

Research the departments and faculty in the area(s) you'll be studying in.

INVESTIGATE JOB CONNECTIONS

Look into the career center and get more information on job fairs, on campus interview opportunities, internships, job placement rate, and the counselor to student ratio.

2

VISIT (OR REVISIT) THE CAMPUS

Take another tour of the school - Just to be sure. Visit while classes are in session, attend a class, or consider spending the night to take full advantage of your visit before possibly enrolling.

3

COMPARE FINANCIAL AID

If you're debating between multiple schools, compare the financial aid awards side by side of your top choices. Understand the free money (scholarships and grants) and money you'll have to pay back (loans).

4

DECISION TIME!

Don't decide overnight, but don't let the time slip away. Colleges are serious about reply deadlines. If you don't send in your deposit on time, you risk losing your place.

ACCEPT

Respond to the college you've decided to attend. Make sure to send in the following items by deadline:
- ☑ Acceptance Letter
- ☑ Separate acceptance letter for financial aid (if required)
- ☑ Deposit

DECLINE

Respond to the college whose offers you're declining. Send a brief note to other colleges and thank them and turn down their offer. This frees up space for other students.

 ## Congratulations! You're In!

- ☑ Take any placement tests
- ☑ Send final official transcript
- ☑ Make any necessary residence hall decisions or preferences
- ☑ Sign up for orientation
- ☑ Register for classes

A brief guide on how to prepare for your college freshman year

Complete the "to-do list" in the college/university portal for the school you will attend in the fall

Registration

- ☐ Select and Register for Fall Classes
- ☐ Register for your school's Pre-Orientation and/or Orientation events
- ☐ Obtain a Parking Permit, if applicable for you Freshman Year

Finance

- ☐ Make sure your Financial Aid is in order. Accept all scholarships and if necessary, accept any student loans offered to you according to your award letter
- ☐ Open a Checking Account and be sure to set up Zelle, Cash App, and/or Venmo

Records

- ☐ Submit your Official High School Final Transcript and any Dual Credit from a Community College or qualifying AP Scores
- ☐ Update and Submit all Immunization/Shot Records to the school you will attend in the fall

Other

- ☐ Set up a college email address for the school you will attend in the fall
- ☐ Complete the Placement Exams if required
- ☐ Make housing deposit, select roommate, and pick a meal plan

Glossary of College Terminology

Academic Calendar: How a school year is divided: usually into three quarters that last from 10-11 weeks, or two semesters that last from 17-18 weeks, or 3 trimesters that usually last about three months each.

Acceptance: Candidate has been admitted, having met the standards set by the college or school.

Accommodations: Upon being found eligible by the Services for Students with Disabilities departments for College Board (SAT and Subject Tests) and ACT, receiving one or more of the following: Extended time, larger print test booklets, permission to bring snacks or mediati on to the test site, extra breaks, sign language interpreter, Braille edition of a test, audiocassette version of a test, a reader to read a test, a writer to record student responses.

Accreditation: Recognition of a college/university by a regional or national accrediting body indicating that the institution has met their standards.

Alumni (plural) Alumna (female singular), Alumnus (male singular): Graduates/graduate of an educational institution.

American College Test (ACT): A standardized achievement test often required for college admissions. The 4-hour test, offered six times annually, covers English, math, reading and science. The highest possible score is 36. (The ACT with writing test, measuring skill in planning and writing a short essay, is required by some colleges).

Advanced Placement (AP): High schools implement AP courses and administer the exams at the end of the school year. College credit is granted dependent upon success on the exam.

Apprenticeship: During a prescribed time period, a worker learns an occupation (usually a trade) in a structured program.

Associate of Arts (AA): A two-year college degree given by community colleges after a prescribed course of study has been completed.

ASVAB: A test that is taken by those wishing to enter the military. This test shows your ability to learn certain skills and your interests. Many schools give this test to their juniors.

Award letter: An official document issued by a college's financial aid office listing all the financial aid awarded to the student. This letter details the analysis of the student's financial need and the breakdown of the financial aid package according to amount, source, and type of aid. The award letter includes the terms and conditions for the financial aid and information about the cost of attendance.

Bachelor's Degree: A degree that is granted after the satisfactory completion of a four-year program of study-usually at a college or university.

Glossary of College Terminology (cont.)

Candidate's Reply Date: At most schools, May 1st is the date by which accepted applicants must indicate their intention to enroll. By use of a common reply date, students may evaluate all notices of admission and financial aid awards before deciding on any one college.

Coalition Application: The online application for more than 150 colleges.

College Entrance Exams: Tests that are used by colleges or universities for evaluation of applicants for admission and/or placement in courses. Tests used most often are SAT, ACT and Accuplacer.

Community College (Junior College): Regionally accredited, post- secondary institution where an associate degree is the highest degree awarded. Certification programs and non -credit courses are also available.

Core classes (CPA): A calculation of grades earned in Math, English, Science, Social Studies, Foreign Language and Fine Arts.

College Admission: Notification from a college or university to which you applied that you have met the necessary requirements and you are accepted.

College Advisor: A staff member or professor who helps a student plan and complete a course of study at a college or university.

College Application: A form that must be completed to be considered for entry into a university, community college, technical school or to be considered for scholarships.

College Board: An organization that sponsors the SAT, the SAT Subject Tests, the Advanced Placement Tests, and the CSS Profile Financial Aid form.

College Coach/Consultant: Private, paid counselors who provide high school students with admissions information, advice, and coaching.

College Fair: A large gathering of college admissions representatives available to speak with prospective applicants, usually sponsored by the National Association of College Admission Counseling in different locations throughout the US.

College Interview: Lasting from 15 minutes to an hour, a meeting between an admissions representative (college official, alumnus or alumna) of a college and a prospective student for the purpose of exchanging information, asking and answering questions, and sometimes evaluating a student's qualifications.

College List: A list of colleges or more that match a student's academic background, as well as his or her intellectual, personal, social, emotional, financial, spiritual, and other needs and desires.

College Preparatory Courses: Courses offered by high schools that meet required or recommended subject requirements necessary for admission to colleges.

Glossary of College Terminology (cont.)

College Representative: An admissions officer assigned to a particular high school, city, or geographic area. This person often is the first admissions official to read a student's application.

College Rankings: Based on different criteria, how colleges measure up against one another as defined by the likes of US News & World Report and others.

College Scholarship Service (CSS) PROFILE: A financial aid form provided by the College Board that is required by many colleges and universities.

College Transfer Courses: Courses intended for transfer of college credit to a bachelor's degree program in a 4-year college or university.

Commencement: A formal graduation ceremony that celebrates recent graduates of the institution with their family and friends.

Common Application: A platform that allows students to apply to approximately 900 colleges that may be filled out and sent to a consortium of member colleges in a more streamlined way instead of submitting each school's individual application. Some colleges also require their own supplemental forms.

Consortium Colleges: A group of colleges that offer joint academic programs, cross-registration for classes, and shared, activity, social, athletic, and other programs.

Cost of Attendance (COA): Price of attending a college for one year.

Course Load: The total number of courses a student is taking per term.

Course of Study: Group of courses students are required to take in order to earn a college degree; a major.

Credit (or Credit Hour): A unit of measurement for fulfilling course requirements. Most colleges require that you complete a certain number in order to graduate.

Class Rank: A student's standing in his/her graduating class that is based on GPA and honors classes. It is expressed in percentages.

Deferment: A period in which student loan repayment is not required.

Deferred Action for Childhood Arrivals (DACA) Program: A kind of administrative relief from deportation. The policy allows young children (under the age of 16) who came to the U.S. without documentation, and have been educated by US school systems, the opportunity to remain in the U.S. by following specific guidelines.

Deferred Admission: The postponing of admission for one year after being accepted into the college or university.

Glossary of College Terminology (cont.)

Demonstrated Need: The difference between a family's contribution as determined on the FAFSA or CSS Profile and the total cost of attending a college.

Denial of Admission Letter: A formal acknowledgment by a college that a student has not been admitted.

Disadvantaged Student: A student who has not had access to the education, background, resources, and services that many other students usually have access.

Doctoral Degree: The most advanced academic degree in most fields. Provides the graduate a high level of expertise and greater options for research, writing, teaching, and management within their specialty.

Dormitories: Campus housing where full-time students live within close distance of the academic buildings.

Dreamers: Individuals who would have qualified under the DREAM Act are often referred to as Dreamers. The term has been used to define individuals in the U.S. who were brought to the country at an early age without documentation but have assimilated to the U.S. culture and have been educated by U.S. school systems. Not all immigrant youth identify as Dreamers.

Dual Enrollment: A student in high school is also taking courses from an institution of higher learning, such as a community college or university. The college classes the student takes typically count toward their high school diploma, as well as college credit.

Early Action: An accelerated application process for certain colleges and universities. Notice of acceptance, denial, or deferment is provided by the school with no obligation to the university to enroll.

Early Admission: A program in which colleges or universities admit outstanding students before the usual admissions date. This can also mean the admission of students before they complete high school.

Early Decision: Many colleges offer this plan to applicants who are sure they want to attend the college. This college should clearly be the applicant's first choice. Traditionally, the deadline for early decision applications has been November 1st or 15th. Colleges then render a decision by mid-December. However, it is common that students will not be informed of their financial aid package at the time they are admitted. If financial aid is a significant issue in choosing a college, applying early decision is NOT to the student's advantage. If accepted under this plan, the student is under strong ethical obligation to attend the college and to withdraw or forego applications to all other colleges.

Early Decision II (EDII): A few colleges offer a second round of Early Decision with due dates in the first part of January and notification usually within six weeks. These are also binding contract programs. Again, students may also be denied or deferred.

Elective: A high school or college course that a student may take, but which is not required to graduate.

Enrollment Status: An indicator of whether you are attending part-time or full-time.

Glossary of College Terminology (cont.)

Entrance Requirements: Also called admission requirements, many colleges require applicants to submit an application, transcripts, and standardized test scores among other materials. Not to be confused with prerequisites.

Expected Family Contribution (EFC): The amount of money the family is expected to contribute to the student's education as determined by a need analysis formula approved by Congress. The EFC includes the parent's contribution and the student's contribution, and depends on the student's dependency status, family status, number of family members in school, taxable and non-taxable income and assets. The EFC is calculated upon submission of the FAFSA form.

Extracurricular Activities: Any formal or informal involvements pursued by students during high school in addition to their regular classes and homework, including sports, volunteer and/or paid work, hobbies, travel, artistic or musical interests, etc. either in or outside of school.

Federal Direct Loan Program: Low interest, subsidized and unsubsidized educational loans made by the federal government to students and parents through the schools. (Also known as Stafford Loans).

Federal Work Study: A federal financial aid program that provides on and off campus work for college students. You qualify for this program through FAFSA.

Federal Student Aid (FSA) ID: A username and password used by current and prospective students and their parents to log into U.S,. Department websites including FAFSA website. The ID is used to sign documents electronically (it has the same legal status as a written signature.

Fee Waiver: An exemption given by a college to disadvantaged students from paying college application fees and ACT/SAT fees based on financial need.

Financial Aid Package: Financial Aid Packages are also referred to as Award Letter, Award Notice, or Financial Aid Offer. Although it is important to note that not all forms of aid included in an offer are awards (that do not have to be paid back such as grants and scholarships). There are different types of aid including loans, work-study, scholarships, and grants. Depending on the package, sometimes it can be cheaper for a student to attend an expensive school because more aid is offered to offset the cost. Therefore, it is important to apply to the schools you want to attend, even if you don't think you can afford it.

First-generation Student: A college student who is the first in their family to go to college.

Fraternities and Sororities: Social and academic organizations for college students formed to pursue a common goal or ideals. Most are identified by letters of the Greek alphabet (Alpha, Beta, Gamma, etc.) and as whole comprise a school's Greek life.

Higher Education: Refers to any formal schooling after high school.

Glossary of College Terminology (cont.)

Four-year University: A postsecondary institution/school that offers undergraduate (bachelor's) degrees. Many four-year universities also offer graduate (master's) degrees.

Free Application for Federal Student Aid (FAFSA): The first step in applying for financial aid in which financial information is gathered from the student and family. It is a form students must file in order to be considered for federal aid programs. There is no fee to apply for federal student aid. FAFSA can be completed online at: www.fafsa.ed.gov.

Full-time Student: A student who enrolls in at least a minimum number (determined by your college or university) of credit hours or courses.

Gap Year: A break in schooling that some students take between high school graduation and their first year of college.

General Education requirements (Breadth requirements): Usually required during the first two years of college, a list of courses from various academic departments that a student must take to graduate.

Grade Point Average (GPA): A calculation of grades earned in coursework.

Grant: Money given by a government or other organization for a particular purpose and does not require repayment.

Greeks: Fraternities and sororities on a college campus. The term "Greek" comes from the Greek letters used as names for organizations (e.g., Alpha Kappa Alpha).

Honors Program: A program that offers an opportunity for students to enrich their educational experience through independent, advanced, or accelerated classes.

Income-Driven Repayment Plan: A loan repayment plan where monthly payments are based on the borrower's income and the number of dependents.

Independent Counselors: Private, paid counselors who provide high school students with admissions information, advice, and coaching.

Independent Study: A program that allows a student to earn college credit through independent study with a faculty member.

Internship: A job in a student's field of study which may be required in some academic programs and may provide salary and/or college credit.

Ivy League: A group of long-established colleges and universities in the eastern U.S. having high academic and social prestige. It includes Harvard, Yale, Princeton, Columbia, Dartmouth, Cornell, Brown, and the University of Pennsylvania.

Job Shadowing: A program by which a student observes employees in a workplace to gain insight about a career or job field.

Glossary of College Terminology (cont.)

Legacy: A college applicant whose parents and/or grandparents have attended a specific college, which sometimes gives them an edge in admissions.

Letter of Recommendation: A letter that supports a student's application to a college for a scholarship. The letter is written by someone who knows you well (not a family member) who can write positively about you.

Loans: Money that is borrowed to pay for higher education and must be paid back with or without interest.

Major Course of Study: A course of study in one subject in which the student specializes in at a college or university.

Master's Degree: An academic degree conferred by a college or university upon those who complete a prescribed study beyond the bachelor's degree.

Merit-Based Aid: Financial aid that is merit-based depends on academic, artistic, or athletic merit, or some other criteria and does not depend on the existence of financial need. Merit-based awards look at grades, test scores, hobbies, and special talents to determine eligibility for scholarships.

Minor Course of Study: A course of study in a secondary subject in which the student specializes in at a college or university. Minors allow students to diversify their courses of study.

Minority: usually referred to individuals from African American, Native American, and Hispanic American backgrounds.

NCAA Clearinghouse: Prospective student-athletes at Division I or II institutions have certain responsibilities to attend to before they may participate. Information concerning who needs to register with the Clearinghouse and what documents should be submitted can be found in the NCAA Guide for the College-Bound Student-Athlete at http://www.ncaapublications.com, or by calling 1-800-638-3731.

NCAA & NAIA: The organizations that certifies athletes for competition in Division I & II intercollegiate athletics.

Need-Blind Admissions Policy: An admission policy that does not take into consideration a student's ability to pay when reviewing his/her application.

Official Transcript: Most colleges will only accept a transcript that bears the high school seal and is sent directly from the high school.

Open Admissions: Students are admitted regardless of academic qualifications and community colleges have an open admission policy.

Glossary of College Terminology (cont.)

Orientation: A meeting/event many colleges offer (hours or days-long) where incoming students and parents/guardians receive information about registering for classes, meet their advisor, and learn about school resources and policies.

Out-of-State Students: Students attending a public university outside of their state. Higher tuition rates may apply until state residency is established.

Parent Plus Loan: The Parent PLUS Loan is a federal student loan available to the parents of dependent undergraduate students. The Parent PLUS Loan offers a fixed interest rate and flexible loan limits. To be eligible, a parent can't have an adverse credit history.

Pell Grant: A federal award given to undergraduate students who demonstrate financial need to help pay for college and it does not have to be paid back. Pell grants are awarded to U.S. citizens and legal residents based on both financial need and timeliness of completing the FAFSA.

Perkins Loan: A campus-administered program that provides low-interest loans to students with exceptionally high financial need.

Placement Test: Colleges and universities may require students to take tests to determine the appropriate level college math and/or English class.

Plagiarism: Taking credit for someone else's work as your own including copying words, sentence structure or ideas. Plagiarism has very grave consequences in higher education.

PLUS Loan: Parents with good credit can borrow up to the full cost of education minus any other financial aid received by the student. According to the law, a financial aid form does not have to be filed to be eligible; however, many lenders require it.

Postsecondary Education: Any education beyond high school, including community college, university, technical school, etc.

Preliminary Scholastic Aptitude Test (PSAT): A practice test for underclassmen to prepare for the SAT. National Merit Scholars are chosen from this test.

Pre-requisite Course: A course or courses that must be successfully completed before a student can enroll in the next level course or more advanced courses.

Preliminary Scholastic Aptitude Test (PSAT): Acts as both a practice test for students who will be taking the SAT for college admissions and as a way for the Collage Board to determine National Merit Scholarship Finalists.

Private College vs. Public College: Public colleges and universities are funded by state governments while private colleges and universities are not publicly owned, often relying on tuition payments and private contributions to operate.

Glossary of College Terminology (cont.)

Probation: Academic probation means a student has fallen from good standing status and is at risk of being dismissed from the university. Institutions measure academic standing by GPA and courses passed. Policies regarding this will vary depending on the institution.

Reserve Officers Training Corps (ROTC): Air Force, Army and Navy programs at the college level that combines military education with bachelor's degree study. A commitment to military service is part of this college program.

Resident: A student who lives in and meets the residency requirements for the state where a public university is located.

Residence Hall/Dormitory: A building on campus that provides on-campus living/sleeping quarters for large numbers of students.

Resume: An outline of your life as a high school student that contains information about your education, jobs, community service and educational and career goals.

Reserve Officers' Training Corps. (ROTC): Program to train college students to become officers in the U.S. Armed Forces.

Rolling Admission:
An admission procedure at some schools, notably larger public universities, in which applications are accepted, evaluated and decided upon as they are received (from as early as September until a final deadline sometime in the spring). This is done on a continuing basis.

Room & Board: The cost or charges stemming from a room in a dormitory and a dining hall meal plan for on-campus food services and housing at a college or university.

Scholastic Aptitude Test (SAT): A college widely used entrance exam that is required by most colleges and universities to measure math and verbal skills. A writing assessment is now optional. The SAT is offered several times a year in the US that includes Critical Reading, Mathematics and Writing sections scored on a scale of 200-800. The total perfect score is 1600.

Scholarship: A merit-based award of money to be used for college costs.

Stafford Loan: A direct federal loan with fixed interest rates.

Subsidized vs. Unsubsidized Loan: If a student receives a subsidized loan, the U.S Department of Education pays all interest accrued during school, the 6-month grace period and deferment. Students with unsubsidized loans must pay interest either while in school or have the accrued interest added to the principal loan balance.

Student Aid Report (SAR): Notifies a student that their FAFSA has been processed. The SAR also may alert you to errors that need to be corrected before money can be awarded.

Glossary of College Terminology (cont.)

Student Loan: Money a student borrows to help pay for college, which must be paid back. Subsidized loans are offered to students who qualify through the FAFSA. The federal government pays the interest while the student is in college. There are also unsubsidized loans where interest begins accruing as soon as the loan is accepted.

Summer Bridge Programs: Programs offered by many universities and some community colleges, which occur in the summer between high school graduation and fall transition to college, which offer students accelerated, focused learning opportunities that can help better prepare them to succeed in college.

Transcript: An official record of high school and/or college courses and grades.

Tuition: The amount of money charged for instruction/classes at postsecondary institutions (see also – cost of attendance).

Undeclared/Undecided: A student enrolled in courses but has not yet declared a major.

Undergraduate Student: A student who has not completed a baccalaureate (usually 4 years) or first professional degree.

Vocational School: A college that provides mostly employment preparation skills for trained labor, such as welding and culinary arts. These programs generally take no more than two years to complete.

Waitlisted: Admissions status that is neither an offer nor rejection. Waitlisted students may be accepted to the college or university later.

Withdraw: To drop a class after the add/drop grace period. Withdrawing often means receiving a W on your transcript.

Work Study: A federal program that provides the opportunity for college students to work part-time jobs (often on the campus of the school they attend) to earn money to pay educational expenses. Students receive compensation in the form of a paycheck, much like a traditional job. Students must submit the FAFSA to be considered for work-study positions.

Yield Rate: The percentage of accepted applicants who enroll in a college compared to the number of acceptances offered.

MECCA College Awareness Post-Assessment

This assessment will help you determine your present level of knowledge regarding some of the topics related to getting ready for college.

Decide how much you agree or disagree with each statement. Circle and write your rating.	Rating Scale		Choose a number on the left to agree or on the right to disagree.			
	Strongly Agree	Agree	Neutral	Disagree	Strongly Disagree	My Rating
I should take challenging courses (including Advanced Placement [AP], Inter-national Baccalaureate [IB] and dual credit and honors if offered.)	5	4	3	2	1	
I am extremely comfortable navigating the college admissions process with little to no assistance.	1	2	3	4	5	
I should stay in contact with my school counselor about resources for college.	5	4	3	2	1	
I plan to apply to one college for admission.	1	2	3	4	5	
I should volunteer and get involved in extracurricular activities.	5	4	3	2	1	
I am familiar with all college applications.	1	2	3	4	5	
I should develop relationships with teachers, coaches, mentors, or other adults, as they will provide recommendation letters.	5	4	3	2	1	
I know I can only apply to colleges and universities using online applications.	1	2	3	4	5	
I should begin early to research scholarships and other funding opportunities.	5	4	3	2	1	
I will only apply to colleges and universities I can afford.	1	2	3	4	5	
Thoroughly research colleges and majors to find the right fit for you and your future career goals.	5	4	3	2	1	
No other materials are required with my college application.	1	2	3	4	5	
Talk to your school counselor about any college fairs or universities visiting your high school or offering virtual fairs.	5	4	3	2	1	
I will need to declare a major before I apply to a college or university.	1	2	3	4	5	
Some applications can be disqualified simply because students do not submit all the required documents.	5	4	3	2	1	
I should apply for financial aid only if I believe I qualify.	1	2	3	4	5	
Seek college application and testing fee waivers from organizations and colleges.	5	4	3	2	1	
My parents' tax return has nothing to do with my dependency status.	1	2	3	4	5	
Create folders (virtual or hard copy) for each college application and/ or create a college application spreadsheet.	5	4	3	2	1	
I should not apply to a college or university if my GPA and ACT/SAT test scores are below the school's entrance requirements.	1	2	3	4	5	
	Add the numbers and write the total.					

90 – 100 **CONFIDENT** about college readiness preparation	70 – 89 **COMFORTABLE** about college readiness preparation	50 – 69 **CURIOUS** about college readiness preparation	0 – 49 **CONFUSED** about college readiness preparation

I Pledge To Be College and Career Ready

I PLEDGE TO:

- ☐ Earn good grades
- ☐ Participate in class
- ☐ Always do my best
- ☐ Complete homework
- ☐ Attend school daily and on time
- ☐ Set goals and work hard to achieve them
- ☐ Ask for help when I need it

BY GOING TO COLLEGE, I WILL:

- **Gain knowledge!** College students acquire skills and expertise in subjects that excite them. They learn how to think critically and express their thoughts.
- **Expand his/her horizons!** College life is full of opportunities to meet new friends, interact with experts in numerous fields and gain hands-on learning and work experiences.
- **Enjoy a secure future!** Higher education is associated with better working conditions, more promotion opportunities and job stability.
- **Have more career options!** Most jobs require education past high school.
- **Earn more money!** A person with a college degree has the potential to earn more money that a person without one.

STUDENT'S NAME: _____

STUDENT'S SIGNATURE: _____

My Child Will Be College and Career Ready

I PLEDGE TO:

- ☐ Support learning at home
- ☐ Make sure my child does his/her best on every test
- ☐ Make sure my child completes his/her homework
- ☐ Make sure my child attends school daily and on time
- ☐ Actively participate at my child's school
- ☐ Help my child set personal goals
- ☐ Teach my child to persevere even when challenges arise

BY GOING TO COLLEGE MY CHILD WILL:

- **Gain knowledge!** College students acquire skills and expertise in subjects that excite them. They learn how to think critically and express their thoughts.
- **Expand his/her horizons!** College life is full of opportunities to meet new friends, interact with experts in numerous fields and gain hands-on learning and work experiences.
- **Enjoy a secure future!** Higher education is associated with better working conditions, more promotion opportunities and job stability.
- **Have more career options!** Most jobs require education past high school.
- **Earn more money!** A person with a college degree has the potential to earn more money that a person without one.

PARENT'S NAME: _____

PARENT'S SIGNATURE: _____

Notes

Notes